Pure Contraption

NED ROREM

Pure Contraption

A COMPOSER'S ESSAYS

Holt, Rinehart and Winston
New York   Chicago   San Francisco

Published simultaneously in Canada by
Holt, Rinehart and Winston of Canada, Limited.

First Edition

Library of Congress Cataloging in Publication Data
Rorem, Ned, 1923–
Pure Contraption.

1. Music—Addresses, essays, lectures.
2. Music—History and criticism.   I.   Title.
ML60.R784P9   780'.8   73–3742
ISBN 0–03–011021–1

Printed in the United States of America

Grateful acknowledgment is made for permission to reprint the
following:

"Pelléas and Pierre" and "Notes on Debussy," *American Record
Guide* (March 1971), copyright © 1971 by American Record
Guide, Inc.

"Notes on Sacred Music," *A.G.O. Music Magazine* (January 1973),
copyright © 1973 by American Guild of Organists, Inc.

"Eliott Carter," copyright © 1972 by Ned Rorem, which first
appeared in *The New Republic* (February 26, 1972), reprinted by
permission of *The New Republic*.

"Smoke Without Fire," copyright © 1972 by Ned Rorem, which
first appeared in *The New Republic* (April 8, 1972), reprinted by
permission of *The New Republic*.

"Paul Bowles," copyright © 1972 by Ned Rorem, which first appeared
under the title of "Come Back Paul Bowles" in *The New Republic*
(April 22, 1972), reprinted by permission of *The New Republic*.

"Lord Byron in Kansas City," copyright © 1972 by Ned Rorem,
which first appeared in *The New Republic* (May 6, 1972), reprinted
by permission of *The New Republic*.

"Stravinsky and Whitman," copyright © 1972 by Ned Rorem, which
first appeared in *The New Republic* (June 3, 1972), reprinted by
permission of *The New Republic*.

To Shirley Gabis Rhoads and Eugene Istomin

Contents

The Composer

All the others translate; the painter sketches
A visible world to love or reject;
Rummaging into his living, the poet fetches
The images out that hurt and connect.

From Life to Art by painstaking adaption,
Relying on us to cover the rift;
Only your notes are pure contraption,
Only your song is an absolute gift.

Pour out your presence, O delight, cascading
The falls of the knee and the weirs of the spine,
Our climate of silence and doubt invading;

You alone, alone, O imaginary song,
Are unable to say an existence is wrong,
And pour out your forgiveness like a wine.

—W. H. AUDEN

Notes from Last Year

The year's ten best concerts? But I've hardly been to any, at least not the kind you make lists about. Oh, I did in fact attend many more than ten musical performances during 1970, but nearly half involved my own compositions with my own participation; the rest were visited from courtesy or from the need to keep up. Not that the season was less excellent than usual, but a composer (especially during a Beethoven centennial) finally feels only waning impulses for the excellence of a Stern or the Stones, Sutherland or Serkin, unless these artists perform his pieces, which they don't.

BERIO'S OPERA

Since all art is revival and nothing is new, revival is new. Depending on who revives what. While Picasso retrieved African sculpture and Stravinsky took to "Neo," John Cage grabbed Dada and made it his own. Or did he? With the new (revived) interest in Dada itself, where can Cage stand? Imitation is the truest form of individuality. Many an *objet trouvé* became identifiably Man Ray's, while Duchamp's moustache on the Gioconda was enough to make her his. And what about Satie, whose plainsong pastiches are plain Satie?

Meanwhile, when Luciano Berio, in *This Means That*, employs as *sonorités trouvées* the Swingle Singers, they remain the Swingle Singers. Berio's well-advertised new work failed by becoming not a scandal but a bore, though the boredom was scandalous. No art is unplanned—certainly none offered to paying publics within confined structures—though some can be irresponsible. Berio's "non-calculations" were miscalculated. With a feeling of having been conned, the not inconsiderable crowd of devotees quit Carnegie Hall, avoiding each other's eyes, after this affair, which appropriately coincided with the season when abortions were legitimized.

As sincerity must be faked to cross footlights, so spontaneity must be rehearsed.

THOMSON'S OPERA

Unstaged scenes from his huge new work *Lord Byron* were formally auditioned and turned down by Bing. Now, Virgil Thomson would be "significant" even were his collaborations with Gertrude Stein not among history's best weddings of words and music: these ingredients *become* each other while remaining separately stylish, sensical, complete: which is more than can be said of (to start from the top) Schubert's collaborations with Wilhelm Müller, or even with Heine. In addition, the wedding resulted not only in song but, on two occasions, in the total theater of opera. *Four Saints in Three Acts* and *The Mother of Us All* can be attended for hours without fatigue.

Of course "best," while not ensuring the thrill of greatness, does guarantee professionality, ever rarer in modern music. Not only should these operas have long since been in the Met repertory, that company ought to have foregone the audition and accepted the new Thomson piece sound unheard. Should it have failed, the Met would have borne less noble failures.

A genius isn't necessarily a talent—Schoenberg for instance. There are verbal musicians who think music more than they feel it.

Might his famous verbal gifts have damaged him as my books may have damaged me, not only to academia, but by usurping the musically creative hours? We can't know what we "would have been if." Composers have always prosified about music (for who would know better?), but without getting stuck, as Thomson has, with the composer-author label. He is not, after all, writing fiction, like composer Paul Bowles. Still, he will probably (has already) become history no less as a reporter of the years 1940 to 1955 than as a musician.

THE LAST SWEET DAYS OF ISAAC

As art this equals *Applause*—"timely" sophomoric gimmicks blown up to last all evening juxtaposed on non-infectious musical pap execrably sung. But whereas *Applause* aims honestly at hicks, *Isaac* poses as a "breakthrough" for connoisseurs, a pose unanimously abetted by Manhattan's drama reviewers. On their advice I spent cash, only to realize for the fiftieth time that musical comedies cannot be trusted to theater specialists. Musically inclined audiences should be warned by knowledgeable music critics against such puerile adventures.

DEBUSSY'S OPERA

The New York City Opera's presentation of *Pelléas et Mélisande* is the best I have ever seen, here or in Paris. Its quality was unquestionably due to the internationality of talents, people who, precisely because they were not French, made a superhuman effort to enter the French brain of the past (of the Dark Ages of Bluebeard, from whom Mélisande had escaped, and of the Paris of 1900, where Claude Debussy lived and loved), an effort not always made by the French who inadvertently sabotage their masterpieces. Frank Corsaro placed the singers in a décor of *art nouveau* (which the French call "modern style") from which New York's Patricia Brooks emerged as an appropriately nubile Mélisande, Canada's André Jobin an unusually masculine Pelléas, while Viennese Julius Rudel conducted the piece like the symphony it is, a violent reverie, an instrumental tissue with words superimposed.

FRANK CORSARO'S DIRECTION

His knack for turning the stalest chestnuts into *marrons glacés* has earned him the position of the City Opera's chief caterer. Yet, when the chips are down, he is more brash than brave. His directorial reputation is based on presenting "other ways" for the tried and true. Even his *Susannah* was a second look at what had become an established staple. To give hypodermics to old war horses is to take safe chances in the public eye: what may be lost in taste and tradition may be gained in energy and acclaim. True risks—those inevitably run by directors of courage—are in new works. Yet one feels that under Corsaro's guidance even a world première would be an alternate version.

SCENARIO

Curtain rises on an exquisite eighteenth-century drawing room. People of quality assemble around a pink keyboard instrument at which is seated a young lady in a powdered wig. She executes an ugly étude in the style of Schoenberg. Everyone smiles, claps politely, withdraws. Curtain falls.

CRITICISM

Love is a puzzle which when solved is forgotten. To scrutinize a heightened experience is to kill it. This no less true of honeymoons than of hallucinogens. And it can be true of art, although art is presumably less ephemeral. Or the scrutiny may itself become art replacing what it kills. Discourse on the current scene often seems subtler, more persuasive, than the scene itself. We read with respectful relish about the qualities of, say, certain obscene books, only to find, when referring directly to them, a dull red herring. The real experience was in discussion of the experience.

FAME

Why do people write books and music?
To become famous.
Not for self-expression?
That need has worn pretty thin by the time they turn professional. Self-expression is primary: making paper dolls or cherry pies. The reward is appreciation, everyone's first need.
Isn't fame a form of appreciation?
Maybe, but appreciation isn't a form of fame. Housewives don't ask to become famous for their cooking, nor husbands for their wheeler-dealing. With an artist, fame can be separate from appreciation, even from understanding (if he's great, how can he be "understood"?). Fame can be divorced from power too, and this is a twentieth-century phenomenon. Rulers of yore thought of glory less than of force, while Bach thought in terms of doing a job. A movie star has less power than the studio chief.

Why is Zsa Zsa Gabor famous? Is she an artist? Can an artist today not be famous? Could he be urged by humanitarian motives? Would he produce if fame were not his goal?
No.
Britten and Salinger shun fame?
They only shun peripheral vulgarities of fame.

TASTE

There is no good taste or bad, there's taste or lack of it. Tasteful versus tasteless. Tasteless as opposed to indiscreet.
Signs posted in European trains describe in four languages the nature of nationalities:

> PRIÈRE DE NE PAS SE PENCHER
>
> E PERICOLOSO SPORGERSI
>
> VERBOTEN
>
> DO NOT LEAN OUT

The French keep within the bounds of taste, and are polite. Italians overflow the bounds, but explain. Germans avoid the bounds, and don't explain. Americans ignore the bounds.
If the worst you might say about a critic is that he lacks taste, the worst you might say about a composer is that he has taste—or only taste. Taste is merely one ingredient of a creative recipe, and is dispensable to many great works. If taste garnishes the music of Rameau, Rossini or Ravel (indeed, the entire Latin sensibility), it is hardly the first element we think of in Beethoven, Strauss or Ives.
Absence of taste is not fatal to an artist as it is to a critic. Taste presupposes a general, that is, comparative, knowledge which any good critic needs. An artist cannot keep up with every trend and still get work done. Which is why Hollywood portraits of The Great depict *gaffeurs* who finally shame everyone by creating their masterpiece. The with-it artist (Lukas Foss, Jean-Louis Barrault) is convincing only

if bandwagons are his normal means of travel. Well-rounded geniuses are as rare as any other kind.

If taste means well-rounded, it means discriminating too, which paradoxically means delimiting. So taste automatically inhibits—again, good for critics, bad for artists. What the latter feel about the former is sheer bemusement, even when highest praises or subtlest diagnoses are offered. Critics find a meaning, then write it down; artists write "it" down, then find a meaning. Meaning, like taste, is a control which comes after the fact.

Creators thus seem narrower and broader than critics. They "know" less, yet of course they know more. Taste isn't their chief concern. Perhaps even intelligence is not a vital requisite for an artist.

MUSIC AS TRANSLATION

The translator's secret lies less in knowing the foreign language than in knowing his own. If we grow aware of how it must have read in the original, if too many locutions appear literally translated, then we are looking through gaping seams upon work poorly done.

A songwriter's secret is the same as a verbal translator's, except that he is not translating from one language into another. He is grafting unrelated media: joining music, which is inherently meaningless in the intellectual sense of the word, to poetry which is inherently meaningful. His success lies less in comprehending the words he is setting than in feeling them musically, and in being able to convince us of the necessity of his feeling.

The various means of grafting are something many composers take for granted but have never written about. I tried, in an essay called "Poetry of Music." Now those poets who read about themselves therein took offense, without exception, as did their friends. The feeling went: "Since Ned treated each one so briefly, couldn't he have been more flattering, or at least more correct?" I was not appraising them as people, or even as poets (if I didn't admire and need their work I'd never have set it to music); I was detailing "collaborations" to illustrate cases. To bring up one poet's concern with billing was not to belittle his art (though is publicity so unartistic?), any more than to say another "supplied" me with verse was to treat him as a pimp (is it wrong to say that Shakespeare, for example, supplies us with poetry?), or to suggest that a third's misreading of the music's intentions was condescending. Actually, all mention of all persons in all contexts is all incomplete and therefore misrepresentative; and even the most accurate mention cannot, in its limitation, jibe with those persons' idea of themselves. To berate me for thumbnail candor while chuckling over the sage ferocity of Stravinsky (how he treats Cocteau, or Copland, even Auden!) is to imply that only the Great have a right to the truth.

Janet Flanner claims that in my description of an evening with her every word was false. To me the words were true, and to (some of) you. No reviewer likes to be reviewed. Her vision of herself is not my vision of her, any more than her Paris is my Paris.

BOOK MUSIC (*Notes for an essay on non-musicians who write about music*)

In his powerful and now-famous story, "Patriotism," Yukio Mishima (like René Crevel in France forty years earlier) previews his own suicide. In the film version made by the author, he considerably weakened (and inadvertently insulted) this detailed act by overlaying it with a soundtrack of the Love-Death from *Tristan und Isolde*. It can't be proved, but probably Mishima's choice of this sumptuous score to illustrate his stark subject was because of Wagner's title rather than his music. The premise: one Love-Death is like another. Even were this true, symbolic interpretations alter every decade. Since programmatic music conveys only what its composer tells you, verbally, it's meant to convey, a Love-Death by any other name would sound as lush. Except for the best ballets, wherein choreography is based on the core of the music, mixed-media ingredients don't mix.

By the same token, books could be written citing great novelists who put their foot in it when talking of music. No other art seems so elusive yet so necessary to cultivated amateurs. Other than Mann, is there one author who incorporated music with an educated intelligence, rather than described it—albeit with awe—as decoration? No, not even Proust. The famous final chapter of *Point Counter Point* comes to mind, but again we find not a musician but a marvelous writer. Gide's book on Chopin resembles Pound's on harmony: their insights become bromides to professional musicians. Sartre and Kafka did not pretend about it, while the surrealists were plain hostile to it.

(Françoise Sagan uses music as furniture: the music of her daily life—the rock of night clubs—actually gives sound to her silent novels, a cut above the filmed biographies of long ago. Can anyone forget Cornel Wilde turning to Merle Oberon, who portrays Madame Sand, and saying, "Say, George"?)

Far from being uncomfortable, American authors are blithe about their ignorance—their indifference—to music. Imagine that non-apologetic attitude about painting! Imagine a composer admitting indifference to books, or a painter to music! Of course, and alas, everyone without embarrassment digs pop.

Even Cocteau, master of all trades, took care to subtitle *Le Coq et l'Arlequin:* "Notes Around Music."
(Ezra Pound: If you want to know X's whereabouts don't go to the F.B.I., look him up in the phone book.)

Suzanne Langer's written smartly about music, but she's not an author, she's a writer—and European, like Forster and G.B.S.
Some who don't care: Philip Roth, Philip Rahv, John Cheever, Mary McCarthy, Norman Podhoretz, Christopher Isherwood. (Isherwood endeared himself to Stravinsky by falling asleep while the music was playing. But musicians do that too.)
Some who do care, but still put their foot—or at least their big toe—in it: Truman Capote, Paul Goodman, Glenway Wescott, Gore Vidal. Truman speaks of sound for its color, as though it were visual. Paul speaks of music (as Auden does) in technical jargon, and so sounds naïve; for artist though he is, he is still an outsider. Glenway writes about the "Emperor Concerto," a second-rate piece, as though it were happening to him, rather than to itself. And take this sentence from Gore's *Two Sisters:*

Of the disappointments of my youth, I recall not so much love affairs gone wrong as those moments of intimacy when at last the dominant theme of the duet was clearly myself, when point counterpoint vain youth and admirer were developing the splendid harmonies of my uniqueness and then, like a non-serial dissonance in a usual work, the music went sour and the other made reference not to me but to self.

No musician could have composed that; the giveaway is "non-serial dissonance . . . etc." Yet I'm willing to bet he wrote it only after consulting a musician.

Less amusing is an "esthetician" like Stanley Burnshaw who balks at voting a book award to Charles Rosen because he (Burnshaw) can't read notes and therefore can't follow the text. By that standard, poems too should be disqualified as too specialized. (No musical example in Rosen's book is beyond a third-grade child with a proper education.)

Gide likened *Les Faux Monnayeurs* to The Art of the Fugue, but it's closer to the Quartet from *Rigoletto*. A fugue, by definition, uses only the same material, which twines around itself in non-differentiated counterpoint. Differentiated counterpoint is what Gide and Verdi use: various themes which twine around each other. A three-voice fugue, for example, resembles a family of identical triplets in perfect agreement, or a madman talking to himself. Gide's book is a symphony, if you will, but certainly not a fugue.

At the end of *Point Counter Point* (which postdates Gide's novel by two years, and emerges from it), Spandrell, while awaiting violent death, converts some friends to the more-than-human persuasions of Beethoven, specially the "Lydian mode" movement of the Quartet Op. 132 in A minor. Huxley's exegesis is original, canny, free of that ingenuous awe one finds in otherwise wise lay musicians. His argument, couched all in non-musical terms, is indeed so "converting" that the fly in that smooth ointment seems the more gross. His record appears to be a 78-rpm of the Budapest played on an old (1928) crank gramophone. Mark and Mary Rampion, hearing *for the first time ever* this complicated quartet, thrill to its "meanings" despite at each record change (roughly every four minutes) a pep talk from Spandrell. Such things don't happen.

They were more likely bored. Masterpieces, even when not accompanied by running commentary, are intrinsically boring: too much goes on, the mind gives way.

To understand a masterpiece is to insult the masterpiece. Huxley uses music for his own purpose. As don't we all.

In *Sunday Bloody Sunday* Ms. Gilliatt, needless to say, uses a trio from *Così fan Tutte* to illustrate her eternal triangle. Why can't intellectuals drop other names than Mozart's? Debussy's say, or Monteverdi's. (They *are* dropping Machaut and Satie now a little.)

Sartre used only an American blues in *La Nausée*. Kafka, nothing: he feared music. Gertrude Stein liked music to "frame" her words. Ditto Tennessee Williams, who speaks of the twelve-tone scale as though it were indeed a scale.

An old fart like Schweitzer lends a meaning to Bach which Bach, historically, could not have comprehended, while nice Jules Feiffer with that worried smile asks me (I'm supposed to know, being a musician) what kind of piece should be used for background in a scene in this movie he's writing where a girl and boy meet in church, Bach, maybe? No, use Messiaen.

One musician's heart sinks on witnessing Allen Ginsberg, presumably oblivious to the TV cameras yet mugging like Dean Martin in slow motion, embedded among acolytes intoning with mindless de-energized redundant unison the stanzas of William Blake. Ginsberg acknowledges he's never studied music, that his settings of Blake are "in a C chord, C major" (he means in a non-modulating Ionian mode; his tonic is actually B-flat), and that he teaches Blake by singing him "because Blake sang, you know—he was a literal poet."

Formal study would not make Ginsberg a better composer, only a discerning one. He needs more of an ear: his music may be fun to join in, as any college songs are for the tone-deaf, but it sounds colorless, uncommunicative, and wrong for Blake, who needs a rainbow blaze. To counter, as Ginsberg does, that although nobody knows what Blake's own music was like, since it was not written down, but that it was "probably similar to what I'm doing . . . (which) is sort of in the style of Isaac Watts" (a hymnodist who died ten years before Blake was born), is not only to strain the credulity of his students, but also to *know* the past, and to assume that an ugly drone is as valid as the simplisticities being droned. Even if we did know Blake's own settings, why set his poems now in the manner of his time rather than ours? Would rock music embellish those poems? Maybe, but rock has its own words.

Couldn't Ginsberg musicalize his own good verses instead? Of course, then he'd risk the inadvertent masochism of a Paul Goodman whose non-professional love for music leads him to believe he's a composer. (Though unlike Pound who turned to Villon—as Ginsberg turns to Blake—Paul sabotages his own perfect poetry.)

COMPOSITIONAL LIMITS

A diary can't contain much humor: that would indicate an objectivity intrinsically absent from diaries. Humor (irony) is also notably absent from the insane, and from children. Most writing is autobiography once removed. So most writers are insane and/or childlike. Does it follow that most masterpieces are humorless?

Until parents are gone we cannot compose freely. Artists compose freely. Yet it's said they are children (and that in becoming adults, artists shed honesty). By nature a child has parents he wants to impress, yet few children are artists. So the syllogism is faulty, unless we state: artists are never orphans; or, inasmuch as only children can be orphans, an artist without mother or father is an orphan, free now, but creating always for his parents.

Does great work come from the loving child of living parents? Does it come, deflowered, the day of their funeral?

If all the children in Kenneth Koch's famous class are poets, then none are. Poetry is more than free-flowing non-literal juices. Poets are exceptional, but the exceptional child is the one without talent.

Optimism is fundamental to intelligence, though pessimism seems fundamental to logic. Saints and artists, at least during business hours, are not sad. Sorrow comes from love and private death, not from science and politics or from failure in these. Such failure is desperate, not sorrowful.

The first philosophy isn't that of suicide, of deciding whether life is worth living, but of deciding the value of writing about whether life is worth living.

An address book takes more wear and tear than a novel. A good one lasts twenty years before coming apart. By then most of those listed have died anyway. Address book manufacturers know this and are fair, exchanging planned obsolescence for well-planned obsolescence.

Great art works, being unique, are final: they do not open doors, they close them.

POLITICS AND PROFESSIONALISM

Auden notes concerning the Renaissance Man: "His attitude is always professional, that is, his first concern is for the nature of the medium and its hidden possibilities: his drawings are drawings, not uncolored paintings, his theater is theater, not reading matter in dialogue. . . ."

But those twentieth-century Renaissance Men who touch on music touch on it as amateurs—Ezra Pound, Jean Cocteau, Lionel Barrymore. Noël Coward's pride in not being able to read music can be considered professional insofar as he "dictates" his notes, though his music's durability is no indication of professionalism in the poet's sense.

Elsewhere Auden states: "I myself do not believe an artist can entirely ignore the claims of the ethical, but in a work of art goodness and truth are subordinate to beauty."

Despite Polonius, truth and beauty aren't necessarily one. Yet people talk of the committed artist, as though commitment (to politics presumably) were a requirement for art, as though the hows and whys of art were choices and not dictates. Commitment will not make an artist special, yet being special is what makes an artist an artist. More relevant than the artist engagé would be the politician engagé who labors so that the state will become committed to art.

There is a difference between what an artist says in his art, and what he says he says in his art. Sure, he can be political, but his politics aren't always in his art. If they are, they shrink or expand into propaganda, because statements about actions are not the same as actions. Actions are more politically effective than rhetoric; an artist's statements are directed to the already convinced, and through his work. His actions are made through his body, in lecture demonstrations

or street demonstrations. Actions may lead to death. Statements never, surely not musical statements.

Music, even bad music, does not inspire ideological behavior. The regular beat of a march may impel men toward
battle, but will it impel them away from battle?

RELEVANCE

Having become a *fait accompli*, the word itself becomes
irrelevant. So far as the arts are concerned the revolution's
won. One's own success is harder than failure to grasp,
especially with the cart before a horse whose committed
heart and body are confused with the creator spirit. We are
all inspired, but we are not all artists. Now that anything
can be said or seen, what do we see and say? The most experimental notion will lie in not being experimental. That
notion could be called daring if the best artists were taking
dares, rather than only breathing, in and out, performing
as they must, not as they should.

All activities relate. Because China concerns America,
America emerges from adolescence into adulthood. The
emergence is communal, therefore Romantic, not Classical,
so the adults look like children. Logically the young are
not occupied with the Classical, nor with contemporary
music of the "classical" or "serious" or "longhair" or "concert" variety. These terms they've invalidated: Classical
means the past; anything good is serious; everyone (except
"serious" composers) wears long hair; and all sorts of music
are played in concert halls. They'd rather make their own
sound than discuss what once was made. And if they do see
formality as pertinent to human feeling, human feeling is
not their target, it being a mirror, reflective, and thus in-
dividualizing. (Exception made for the community reflection of Quaker Meeting.) They'd rather shriek together,
for shrieks are Now. (That last sentence, by the time it is
read, may sound more like a whimper than a bang. When

people ask, as they always do, what is the future of music? the only answer is, which future? five minutes or fifty years from now? Music alters during the time it takes to ask the question.)

That Classical music seems irrelevant to most young people of today is a truism: it's always been irrelevant to most young people as to most people, not because it doesn't obtain to the moment, but because it obtains only for certain sensibilities, and even for such sensibilities it's hard.

Complication for itself is one effect of decadence. For the first time we are seeing decadence as simplification for itself.

By 1960 concert music had become such a Gordian knot that composers couldn't actually hear what they had notated. Whereupon pop cultists, not even slicing the knot because they didn't know it was there, drowned out these composers with songs so fresh that even jazz by comparison sounded muddy. Today the freshness has hardened into irresistible commerce: old Bach specialists update their "product" with light shows, while middle-aged composers simplistify themselves for the common denominator. The common denominator couldn't care less, having its own musicians who are geniuses—because they make more money.

My sole advice to the young: choose well from whom you steal.

The young who are talented and beautiful come to learn from us who are only talented. We admire their beauty. They resent the admiration and withhold their beauty. Must we admire their talent? Can't they learn, just from the fact of us? We love them for themselves alone, and they complain, the little shits.

Mature cannot contrast with Young, since Young can be Mature. Invention has always come from youths, many of whom completed their life's work, or the best of it, before twenty-one. Lautréamont, Rimbaud, Radiguet. Cultural power, in the sense of artistic creativity, has always been in the hands of the young—the young individual. But oh, the young group! I would live in terror of the young taking over the world, except for what the old have done to that same world.

Young artists who refute the past do have a point, although irrelevant is a mere catchword to define the unknown. Shakespeare *is* irrelevant to our present (surprisingly relevant too). But art is imagination, not slogan. A Cranach nude, a Monteverdi madrigal were no more pertinent to their periods, politically or socially, than a Balthus nude, a Webern madrigal today. In art questions of pertinence are impertinent.

Where does the past begin? With the year 1066 or with our previous generation? With the early works of Boulez or with a song Bob Dylan wrote this morning? Merely to live from day to day is to break with the past. To perform music of the past is to sever relations with the past, since our *sound* would be unrecognizable to the original composer. The sound of today is whatever is sounded today.

The past is irretrievable in any case, as Borges is not the first to point out. Should a man rewrite *Don Quixote* simply by copying the original, his work would belong to himself, not Cervantes. Revisiting the unaltered scenes of childhood we find a lake of tears in which we, who feel unaltered, perceive our unrecognizable reflection.

MOVIE MUSIC

Mixed media? What else is the Catholic mass? Or opera? True, in musical circles the expression is understood to include colored lights. Longtime conservative composers who now turn to this expression are put off by public reaction: they used to be told how beautiful their music sounded; now people come up after a concert to say how heavenly it looked.

Not that the visual is stronger than the aural, it is just more obvious (the eye's a less ambiguous mechanism than the ear), and musicians can choose to bathe in the obvious. Yet such is music's hidden power that it can render a bad movie acceptable, whereas a good movie cannot rescue a second-rate score. Elio Petri's engrossing film, *Investigation of a Citizen Above Suspicion*, was undermined for at least one viewer by a background of pseudo-Weillian treacle, while a return visit to the beloved *La Belle et la Bête* proved that Cocteau, a trend-setter for three generations, had his defenses down the day he allowed Auric to spew all over his images with an unceasing Heavenly Voices–type sound. On the other hand, how would *Of Mice and Men* hold up today, or *The Heiress*, without the poignant dimension added by Copland's special noises? Meanwhile, there are white elephants (though how many?), like *Le Sacre du Printemps*, which trample all comers, from Nijinsky through Disney to Béjart.

Opponents of movies-as-art ask how often you go back to see your Great Film, as though only repetition with its intimations of idolatry proved grandeur. (I, for one, have seen many a lousy film many times.) Well how often do we return to see great plays? Do we reread Balzac and Tolstoy much? How often have the Opponents read James complete? The fact is, to re-experience anything is to provide a novelty worth noting. Anything, except music.

We are not considered novel, or maniacal, when we listen to a record of Ravel's *L'Enfant et les sortilèges* thirty times a week, or see Verdi's *Don Carlo* seventeen times with seventeen casts, or study Beethoven's last quartets daily for decades. For if books may be sensually mulled in retrospect without ever directly consulting them again, the pleasure in music recalled is virtually non-existent. Music must be reheard to be re-experienced.

MODERN MUSIC

Yesterday the phrase meant what serious live musicians were up to. The phrase was so self-evident that when laymen at parties asked a composer "Do you write modern music?" what they really wondered (any music of the present being by definition modern) was, "Do you write Stravinskyish noise, or like Bach, or maybe Grieg?" Under no circumstances did they mean jazz, because a jazz composer wouldn't be at the same party. Today modern music means pop, pop having achieved dignity for all strata of international society who no longer need to pretend to like classical. The old meaning has atrophied except for a handful of specialists.

ART SONG

What is it?, people occasionally ask, seeing my name linked to the term. The term's not in my vocabulary. Is Art Song art any more than Grand Opera's grand? It is our feeble translation of the French *mélodie* or the German *lied*, to distinguish the genre from pop. The genre once referred to settings of pre-existing poetry, to be sung by a trained voice under the formal circumstances of a recital. Today the rise in quality of some pop, and the increasing rarity of the formal recital (though the rise and rarity must not be mistaken for fusion), suggest that Classical and Popular—or Sacred and Profane—need re-differentiation as

Commercial and Non-commercial. Thus the songs of, say, Mancini, Bacharach, Lennon, Jagger, are commercial; non-commercial are those of, say, Virgil Thomson, David Diamond, Paul Bowles, Richard Cumming. Of itself salability need not imply less good or less genuine. Still, however heartfelt the songs of Bacharach, they delight his publisher mostly for their mass consumption potential; and however original the songs of Bowles, they draw from his publisher only this sigh: "Another prestige item!"

The two musics have always simultaneously served two needs, and indeed, until lately, two kinds of people, of which the majority always prefers pop, hence the name.

INTERVIEWS

One trouble with interviews as information (beyond the notorious fact that biography is drenched in the biographer's prejudices) is that the choicest nuggets are unearthed once the meeting is over. Presumably. Or else the interviewee talks and talks, reformulating for the thousandth time those formulas which, by virtue of repetition, he no longer questions. Talks and talks, like Anna de Noailles, precisely to dissimulate the fact that which makes him lies not in speech but in work. I don't says this necessarily of non-creative personalities like Pablo Casals or Carol Channing, but of myself. I talk because I've nothing to say, because my intelligence is no more than itself, filling an empty shell.

POSTLUDE

To be moved by music anymore! For we are usually moved by association: by the words to Our Song from high school, by visuals (the ballet sight recalls former Prince Igors), and, for me, even the odor of Russian Leather revives old sounds. How, though, does "pure" or so-called abstract music move us, a Beethoven quartet, a non-programmatic Debussy sonata, indeed any non-vocal piece which doesn't pretend to tell a story? Does it provoke us sexually? inspire tears? make us sick?

Sick? Once when our friend the musician Noah Greenberg was presenting *The Play of Daniel*, we went to see and hear it at the Chapel of the Intercession. Midway through, one of the twelve angelic choir boys began to vomit, copiously, in view of hundreds, all over his white robes and the altar steps. While cymbals and trumpets continued inviolably, an older angel helped him beneath her wing into the corridors, hiding his humiliation and physical pain. Meanwhile not even the strewing of sawdust on the puddle of puke could quash the stench rising stronger than incense through the church to remind us that the boy's emotion toward this theatrical reality had moved us more than the music pure.

Now, could the child have reacted thus to a *straight* piece, without God, or choruses, or superimposed "meaning," or above all, without his direct participation?

January 1971

Elliott Carter

The art of Elliott Carter understandably provokes contrasting attitudes. Some who know and care contend wistfully that he is the last great master; others, mostly from among the young, feel that if the species is dying it's no loss to them. Harold Schonberg, usually outspokenly contemptuous of all categories of new music, remains deferential in his dislike of Carter, while Virgil Thomson says, "Carter's chamber music is the most interesting being composed today by anyone anywhere," and John Simon bizarrely suggests that Carter (whose experience with and interest in the sung word is avowedly edgy) could be the savior of American musical comedy. Meanwhile his detractors find in this composer a subtle parvenu.

If a master is one who writes masterpieces, who aims high and hits the mark using as weapon the Big Statement (a piece inherently long and with profound intent, like the post-Beethoven sonata forms, as opposed to inherently short pieces like Webern's), then Elliott Carter fills the bill. But it is true that the Big Statement, descending as it does from nineteenth-century preoccupations, has indeed grown extinct, the victim of gigantism, at least in purely instrumental repertories. (Most of the important gestures of the so-called serious music world, and all of them from the pop world, have, since *Le Sacre du Printemps* in 1912, involved the human voice.) Carter is the only composer after Bartók who can make a convincing Big Statement in non-vocal mediums, particularly in the otherwise atrophied string quartet. He stands isolated in his mastery, as much through uniqueness of viewpoint as through genius.

This singular position was gained neither easily nor early. Born in 1908, Carter did not settle into himself until his mid-forties. Before that his music sounded rather commonplace —not in the sense of vulgar, which can be thrilling (like Gershwin as contrasted with Cole Porter, or Weill as contrasted with Reynaldo Hahn), but in the sense of second-rate, which can be dull (like all those neo-classical composers as contrasted with Stravinsky). Carter's composition of the 1930s and early 1940s was of the "accessible" Coplandesque brand; he felt "a social responsibility to write interesting, direct, easily understood music." Had this music in fact been "interesting" or, more important, successful in its day, one wonders where Carter might be now. Around 1950 he made the intellectual decision to focus, as he puts it, "on 'advanced' music, and to follow out with a minimal concern for their reception, [his] own musical thoughts along these lines. . . . If a composer has been well taught and has had experience," Carter adds about himself, "then his private judgment of comprehensibility and quality is what he must rely on if he is to communicate importantly."

He was communicating importantly enough by 1955 to have replaced Aaron Copland as national father figure, and to be the only American taken seriously on their terms by the élite of European composers. And though he jumps through no hoops, his position remains secure in 1972 when half of being an artist lies in self-promotion. Like Roger Sessions, he has never pushed his persona along with his product, a stance nearly as anachronistic as his choice of musical terrain. If for no other virtue than integrity, Elliott Carter at sixty-four finally deserves a book-length study. *Flawed Words and Stubborn Sounds* is not, however, it.

Although more than three-fourths of the volume consists of an edited transcript of Carter's replies to queries posed by one Allen Edwards, the result seems somehow unauthentic. Edwards has chosen not only the format but (pathetically) the tone of the famous Stravinsky-Craft *Conversations*. He has proceeded on the assumption that his subject is "a composer I know I am not alone in regarding as the most important to have appeared in America," and then exempts himself from literary responsibility ("The defects that remain in the final text are ones for which I am motivated to ask the reader's indulgence because of my conviction of the overriding value of the perspective here gained"). From the painful ejection of the very first question the book sags, for the protagonists lack the Craft-Stravinsky gift of gab; their scholarly exchange does not of itself result in the literature that should be the one excuse for this kind of publication. Mr. Edwards depicts the two of them in an ivory tower of Babel satirizing a situation which Carter in reality deplores.

Not even by comparison can Elliott Carter come to life, except in a few instances of anecdotage (for example, a description marked by admiring tenderness for Nadia Boulanger), or of working method. This is to be pitied, because Carter's answers often contain ideas, explanations, and recollections which in their present raw form could be transformed into an excellent *written* (not transcribed) book. His comments on American education provide a most attractive indictment of a system which at every turn stifles the imagination, preaches a materialistic concept of success, and advocates allegiance to an often narrow vision of The American Way. But his youthful friendships with Ives,

Whitehead, Ralph Kirkpatrick, and other fabulous greats are alluded to only teasingly, as though "personal" discussion would soil the higher purposes in question. His pessimistic appraisal of what a composer can expect by way of public acclaim and respect might make some impress on the public conscience were it tightened into a formal essay. And surely he has more to say about the problems of vocal composition than the meager half page allotted to it.

Elliott Carter's ideas about his own music, reduced to lowest terms, are neither complicated nor especially original (his notions about orchestration, for instance, or the celebrated "invention" called metric modulation), but they are necessarily valuable as statements by a vital artist "in process." Perhaps one day he'll authorize a less pompous biography, or, better still, collect his own thoughts in essay form. Despite what Edwards declares in his foreword, Elliott Carter surely has time for this. Any artist does.

The title from Wallace Stevens seems inappropriate. Despite Carter's modesty (in one footnote he refers to this complex theoretical exchange as "bits of useful information [which] may help a few readers to understand something about what it is for one person, at least, to write music in the United States"), his own words are not really flawed, except inasmuch as any discussion of art, however complete and learned, becomes *de trop* before the fact. Nor are his musical sounds at all stubborn, although his endless compositional patience might be so termed. But even the best books on music can only demonstrate points, while music itself proves points. On closing this book we ache from structure-talk and long for living notes—for what the same Wallace Stevens called *Not Ideas About the Thing But the Thing Itself.*

January 1972

The Classical Style

It is harder to review a good book than a bad one. Beyond offering a résumé and a definition, what can a reviewer say that the author hasn't said better? This is especially true in the present case when the book itself is a résumé and a definition: in one sense *The Classical Style* provides its own review. Still, it is not the book's high quality but a generic quandary that inhibits me.

Surely editorial policies fluctuate about who writes up what: should women review women's books? should blacks review blacks? Or musicians musicians? Why not? if the critic knows what the author is talking about. The trouble is, there are as many kinds of musicians as there are women or blacks.

We inhabit distant worlds, Charles Rosen and I. Though both musicians, he is a classical scholar, I a contemporary composer. He seems obsessed with analysis, not only his own but that of others, judging by his discussion in *The New York Review of Books* of certain literary and musical specialists, past and present, who expound about the number of angels that can dance on a pinpoint. Painstakingly he would render tangible that which with me is unconscious and assumed: the principle of *métier*. Essays centering upon the force and form of creation, whether they inspire the special pedantry of a William S. Newman, whose monumental series on the Sonata suggests six thousand footnotes in search of a text, or the unusual pedagogy of a Sir Donald Tovey, whose literary skill rivals a true maestro's baton, are all (once résumé and definition get settled) after one thing: the secret of greatness. Such essays never prove conclusive, but while their subject continues to beguile both pedagogue and layman, it remains indifferent to artists themselves: the meaning of greatness is not an artistic concern. Artists are less interested in how something came to be than in bringing something to be.

Certainly as a composer I am more enlivened by writing music than by reading about writing music. When occasionally I see program notes regarding my own music I am struck with how correct they are in detail, yet as a whole they never hit the unseen nail on the head. If their annotator reveals, even to me, some convoluted nuance in the score, I'm more touched than instructed by his care and wonder why he bothered. Now although this very stance could arm me with a viewpoint toward music's structuring, it would lack insight, for by definition I'm on the inside looking out. Charles Rosen speaks from a reverse position and knows "about" music far more than I.

He would be the first to appreciate the disparity between musicological and creative approaches, as when he writes: "Reading a composer's mind, retracing the steps by which he worked, is not a viable critical method even when the composer is alive and one can ask him how he did it—he generally does not know."

There are as many kinds of people who write about music as there are those who write about the writing. Three key types are the daily reviewer who explains the When, the analytic critic who explains the Why, and the practicing composer who explains the How. There are dozens of combinations of these. One thinks immediately of Schumann, Berlioz, Debussy, Schoenberg, Sessions, Thomson, Hindemith, all first-rank composers, all first-rank critics, some of whom earned at least part of their living as reviewers. One thinks of non-practicing musicians who are authorities like Alfred Einstein and Paul Henry Lang, or popularizers like David Ewen and Joseph Machlis. Other professional authorities are not musicians at all, G. B. Shaw, E. M. Forster, Brigid Brophy. Certain amateurs pretend to discuss music professionally, albeit with no authority, like Gide in his booklet on Chopin, or Pound in his treatise on Harmony, naïve statements from authors who learned the hard way (that is, away from class) what the most casual music student takes for granted. Poets like Auden in his souvenirs of *The Rake's Progress* or John Hollander in *The Untuning of the Sky* write on music with technical know-how, while others bring us "poetic" *précis* on composers—Frank O'Hara on Morton Feldman or Paul Éluard on *Les Six*. Naturally there are novelists who use music intrinsically for character portrayal, as Mann in *Doctor Faustus* and Rolland in *Jean Christophe*, or extrinsically like animated wallpaper, as Proust throughout his big book or Huxley in *Point Counter Point*.

Finally there are executant musicians such as Lotte Lehmann or E. Robert Schmitz who publish practical manuals on how to perform. But there is the performer who is also the scholar. In North America have been Glenn Gould, Robert Craft, Ralph Kirkpatrick, and more recently Charles Rosen combining the virtues and none of the vices of the above categories.

First-generation North American pianists are comparatively young, around forty-five or fifty. A notable preceding generation does not, for whatever reason, exist; the mentors of this first generation were at least twenty-five years older and inevitably Central European with a repertory built on the eighteenth- and nineteenth-century masterworks. Reaching their twenties, the pupils spread wings and, more often than coincidence allows, flew to France. Their attraction to that country grew in general from a sharing of the postwar syndrome of American youth seeking "roots" in the now defertilized pastures of Sartre and Jean Gabin, and grew in particular as an antidote to their intensely German-focused training. For varying periods they centered in Paris, some even becoming French scholars: Julius Katchen, Leon Fleisher, Jerome Lowenthal, Eugene Istomin, Gary Graffman, Alexis Weissenberg (though not William Kapell or William Masselos, special cases and slightly older).

With all their basking in especially the literary, visual, and culinary aspects of the culture of France, their musical tastes still remain true to their Jewish-American origins, meaning to Germany and Austria (although in the 1940s and 1950s they were understandably not tempted by the hospitality of these lands). All continued to feature the standard repertory of the three B's, with hardly a gesture toward Ravel, much less toward Franck, and none at all toward American music.

(A waspier generation of pianists in their thirties, exemplified by John Browning and Van Cliburn, is no less German-masterpiece–prone, but without pretense to a French living style. Nor is expatriation a notion any more occurring to today's very young performers in the United States.)

Again Charles Rosen, born 1927 in New York City, is both an issue of and exception to the above generalities. It is interesting to remember that he received his doctorate in French literature, and has been recognized for twenty years not only as a virtuoso of French piano music of the so-called Impressionist era (his recording of Debussy's "Études" being exemplary) but of modern American music. He and the harpsichordist Ralph Kirkpatrick were the creators of the "Double Concerto" by Elliott Carter to whom *The Classical Style* is dedicated. Now if what we call classical can be applied to a school of French literature, it was virtually non-existent in French music. Musical classicism originated, developed, and decayed in the Germany of the late eighteenth century. Rosen thus may be said to straddle three continents in both space and time, and to convince us that he is professionally at home in them all, a posture I cannot begin to comprehend and am in awe of.

To understand all about a language except how to speak it, to get everything except the point, here are the frailties of historians! The classical masters resuscitated might grasp what researchers wisely write of them, but only after the writing was "translated," as one explains sight to the blind, or his own illness to a patient. Still, such explanations account for all but the essential, nor is there any one way of listening. A good piece encases more than even its composer knows; what we find in it depends on how we've got our ears screwed on. Anything can signify anything, and research travels ever far and clear. Virgil Thomson maintains that we can now cast a floodlight onto the past and illuminate our knowledge of performance in all details except one —what it meant to the people of the time.

The rarest qualities of Rosen the researcher are his good writing and his concern with sound.

His opinions about his vast store of information he expresses with professional economy and contagious devotion. That most musicologists (or music historians, as some prefer to be called) are mere compilers without style is no surprise, but that they seem more preoccupied with how music looks than with how it sounds may come as a contradiction to many laymen. Rosen seldom errs in that direction; he reacts to music through the ear (to how form is derived from sound, not vice versa), and his words evoke not only the arch of a tune which, after all, must change according to the soprano or viola or bassoon emitting it, but of those sensual vertical textures planned orchestrally by the composer. Moreover, he comes as close as anyone to entering the composer's heart and head and uttering what the composer doesn't "know." And yet . . .

The foregoing skirts the actual contents of Charles Rosen's book, although the margins of my copy seethe with penciled notes. Their nature is at once so obvious and so specialized as to be useless to any reader of reviews. Obvious, because I learned from *The Classical Style* exactly what any non-musician would learn; but I dare not divulge what I learned without sounding the fool, for I couldn't make comparisons to other books of this kind, never having read any. Specialized, because I take exception to the meaning (i.e., the cause of the persuasive value) proposed by Rosen for every example he cites in his numerous analyses; but my exceptions are esthetic, based on personal method, unprovable, and I'm no more right than he.

All my life I've been on close terms with much of the music discussed here so elegantly. But I played it unconsciously, for it never occurred to me *not* to understand what the notes "meant," nor to wonder at the numerous *trouvailles*, while Rosen, quite consciously and with no end of skill, has placed himself in the composer's seat. When he himself states that a composer "wants his intentions made audible, not his calculations," I realize that I've always linked the two unquestionably and cannot help but find such vast amounts of diagnosis a bit—well—superfluous.

In short, insofar as this book is involved, Rosen and I face opposite directions, the past and the future, so I'm incapable of having an attitude toward his work. I cannot, so to speak, face it.

March 1971

Paul Bowles

In 1949, with the publication of his very successful *Sheltering Sky* at the age of forty, Paul Bowles became the author-who-also-writes-music, after having long been the composer-who-also-writes-words. That success brought more than a re-emphasis of reputation; from the musical community's standpoint it signaled the permanent divorce of a pair of careers. During the next two decades Paul Bowles produced fourteen books of various kinds, but little more than an hour's worth of music. Did he feel that one art, to survive, needed to swallow and forget the other? Surely he received in a year more acclaim for his novel than he had received in a lifetime for his music. This need not imply a superior literary talent; indeed, if history recalls him, it will be for musical gifts. It's just that ten times more people read books than go to concerts. Someday Bowles may fully release the underestimated musician who doubtless still sings within him. Meanwhile, perhaps chagrined by the underestimation, he coolly enjoys an international fame based solely on his books.

Composer-authors generally compartmentalize their two vocations, allotting parts of each year, if not each day, to each profession. But as authors their subject is inevitably music (as witness Berlioz, Schumann, Debussy, or today, Boulez, Thomson, Sessions), whereas Paul Bowles is a fiction-writing composer, the only significant one since Richard Wagner, and even Wagner's fiction was at the service of his operas. Except during the war years when he functioned as music critic for the *New York Herald-Tribune*, Bowles' prose has been antithetical to his music. Whatever resemblance exists between the working procedures for each craft, the difference between his results is like day and night.

Paul Bowles' music is nostalgic and witty, evoking the times and places of its conception—France, America, and Morocco during the Twenties, Thirties, and Forties—through languorous triple meters, hot jazz, and Arabic sonorities. Like most nostalgic and witty music that works, Bowles' is all in short forms, vocal settings or instrumental suites. Even his two operas on Lorca texts are really garlands of songs tied together by spoken words. In 1936 Orson Welles' production of *Horse Eats Hat* became the first of some two dozen plays for which he provided the most distinguished incidental scores of the period. The theater accounts for a huge percentage of his musical output, and for the milieu he frequented for a quarter of a century, most latterly the milieu of Tennessee Williams whose works would never have had quite the same tonality—the same fragrance—without Bowles' music emerging from them so pleasingly. Indeed, the intent of his music in all forms is to please, and to please through light colors and gentle textures and amusing rhythms, novel for their time, and quite lean, like their author.

Paul Bowles' fiction is dark and cruel, clearly meant to horrify in an impersonal sort of way. It often bizarrely details the humiliation and downfall of quite ordinary people, as though their very banality was deserving of punishment. Bowles develops such themes at length and with a far surer hand than in, say, his sonata structures. His formats in even the shorter stories are on a grander plan than in his music; at their weakest they persuasively elaborate their plots (albeit around ciphers, and in a style sometimes willfully cheap); at their best they transport the reader through brand-new dimensions to nightmare geographies. Bowles communicates the incommunicable. But even at their most humane his tales steer clear of the "human," the romantic, while his music can be downright sentimental. Indeed, so dissimilar are his two talents that it is hard to imagine him composing backgrounds to his own dramas.

Paul Bowles' real life is courageous and exotic. Whenever possible he has spent it in what we like to call backward countries with hot climates, especially Ceylon and North Africa. Yet no matter how far afield he has wandered into the crowds of India or the deserted Sahara, he has maintained active correspondence with the West, specifically with American intellectuals who, since he seldom goes to them, cross oceans to meet him. Bowles, the social animal, has traveled Everywhere, known Everyone, and been much loved. His writings have dealt extensively with the Everywhere, but never until recently with the Everyone. Now here is his autobiography.

Without Stopping is curiously static but never tranquil, like Lewis Carroll's Red Queen. If in reality the author withdraws for long years of disciplined reflection in faraway lands, the effect from his book is of constant and vaguely futile comings and goings. *Without Stopping* is also curiously reticent, at least for a volume of memoirs. Obviously uncomfortable with the pronoun "I," the autobiographer is revealed as far less rich and strange than the actual man. Here he denigrates his subject's "specialness." Scores of names are dropped with no further identification than their spelling, while close acquaintants vanish and die without so much as an editorial sigh from their friend. He displays no envy of competitors, no sign of carnal or intellectual passion. His one obsession would seem to be for investigation—not of the heart, which even his fiction avoids, but of the body as affected by foreign cultures, by the implacability of nature, exotic cuisine, ill health, hard drugs, but never, never by sex. If his novelist's reputation qualifies this printing of his journal, his novelist's morosely powerful voice remains mute. Occasionally we find a discussion, always objective, of literary method, but never of musical method. And his reticence rather grandly forbids display of the self-doubt which is an artist's *sine qua non*. Yet since Bowles is an artist, he is allowed his own rules. More than once he mentions his revulsion at the artist's visibility, be it through old-fashioned bohemianism or modern publicity. (On first meeting Stephen Spender in 1931: "I noted with disapproval the Byronesque manner in which he wore his shirt, open down to his chest. It struck me as unheard of that he should want to announce his status as a poet rather than dissimulate it; to my way of thinking he sacrificed his anonymity.") Why, then, write a book of this sort?

Could anyone not knowing Paul Bowles have the least interest in such a report? Maybe. Once we accept our disappointment at the low gossip content and learn that the work is a cold fulfillment of a commission more than an inspiration, we can enjoy the elliptical levels of the writing. With the assurance of an aristocrat the author presupposes our acquaintance with his friends, with the books he likes, and with his own books and music and multilingual abilities. He assumes our knowledge of Jane Bowles' extraordinary creation, and, as with the subject of marital affection, deems it more tantalizing, and thus more skillful, not to spell things out. As for the heart, others have bled it to death, so why should Paul Bowles? when the description of a jackal's wail or a Jalila trance or a Ceylonese temple filled with bats can be more terribly thrilling.

Still, the final crabbed product comes to less than the sum of its parts. The best of what is written here has been better written elsewhere by another Paul Bowles: the verbal landscapes. If he is not a human portraitist, he has, like some filmmakers, created character from scenery. Deserts, jungles, city streets are personages in his books as in his life, and he causes them to breathe and suffer and threaten us as only a god can do. But when discussing real people the effect is desperate, touching, even sad, sometimes humorous, though only secondarily the effect he intended, that is, a pose of non-involvement. That effect, which fills the novels, no longer seems viable for our troubled world—perhaps precisely because the world has turned into a Paul Bowles novel.

The best of Paul Bowles' early music contained a high-class appeal uniquely his own. Appeal has come to be considered a negligible ingredient in music. It would be interesting to see if Bowles could revive it, or if not, what dialect he might sing should he choose to sing again. The general public has forgotten his music, forgotten even that he was—is—a composer (our shyest composers must hustle ever more crassly to keep themselves known). Paul Bowles however has a built-in literary public who would receive warmly whatever he does. Let him finally reconcile his talents. For his music has had a long nap and might wake up refreshed, whereas his prose in this book seems momentarily exhausted.

April 1972

Great Songs of the Sixties

Here is a book that should interest our Vice President whose recent attacks on today's popular music have made headlines. This anthology of eighty-two songs which "ignited" our youth during the past decade offers a heady mixture of commercial exploitation and cultural documentation.

The music, attractively engraved on high-quality stock, is prefaced with an analysis of Sixties popular song by editor Milton Okun, introduced with an essay by Tom Wicker, and visually enhanced with eighty-four pictures of Sixties people and events, the whole sturdily bound in a loose-leaf plastic binder. Such a classy product, clearly aimed at the mass market (an affluent one, judging by the high price), should appeal primarily to an older generation that both reads a little piano and likes some of the tunes, yet found the Sixties sound mostly unpalatable.

Tom Wicker's introductory essay juxtaposes the various stresses and moods of the past decade with compassionate intelligence. He feels that the governing principle of the Sixties was change, often of a violent kind. Since change touched every socio-cultural aspect of that period (technological and economic developments having revolutionized man's basic processes), it necessarily touched the arts. Wicker's observations that "much of the music of the Sixties hangs on some aspect of change," and that Agnew saw "the 'revolution' of the Sixties as a menace to American traditions, democratic ideals, and property values," go far in explaining the underlying anger of the Vice President's attitude toward this music. But it is Wicker's discussion of the contradictions of the Sixties, and not of the music (or rather the lyrics) to which he only passingly refers, that makes his essay valuable.

Unfortunately, Milton Okun's preface is not only too extravagant for value ("The songs of Dylan in this collection include the two most important political statements of the decade") but largely consists of false comparisons at the expense of pre-Sixties pop song. For example, he states that while the music of the Sixties reverberated with genius and talent as never before, "craftsmen like the Gershwins, Porter, Kern, Hammerstein, Rodgers and Hart, Harburg, and Berlin . . . dealt with a single emotion—romantic love—in a way that seems superficial and impersonal. The young Sixties generation, on the other hand, was desperately concerned with the quality of life—and this concern marked the departure of popular music from sentimentality to hard reality."

But even as songs of the Sixties expressed many concerns, for each "hard reality" *The Times They Are A-Changin'* any buff can recite *My Forgotten Man, Love for Sale,* or *Brother Can You Spare a Dime?,* not to mention Weill and Brecht or Woody Guthrie. And numerous examples abound in the music of those "craftsmen" which show them as concerned with the "quality of life" in their time as is Dylan in his. If most of the songs of the past dealt with "romantic love" (excluding the *My Heart Belongs to Daddy* variety), a peek at the table of contents of this collection

reveals listings for several dozen oozing with the same sentimentality Okun professes to scorn.

He also reports that the most important influence on
song of the last decade was Negro music, "previously outside the ken of popular song." Forget all blues, all jazz, Bessie Smith and Ethel Waters, even Al Jolson whose singing
was no less a caricature of black sound than is Mick Jagger's. Finally, with the statement that only in the Sixties did
people sing "as they really felt" (were Billie Holiday, Judy
Garland, Mahalia Jackson, Louis Armstrong, even Peggy
Lee mere hacks?), Okun resembles the huckster who dis-
claims the ingredients of any product not his own.

But it is "great songs" rather than prose which cover the
more than 300 pages of this volume. Now to suggest that
eighty-two of anything from any decade can be great, let
alone from the still-warm Sixties, is risky. As used here,
great denotes the editor's preferences rather than signaling
any special quality or even popularity, since hits from *Hello
Dolly!* or by The Jefferson Airplane aren't included.

Nor is there a single example of art song, certainly a
major genre. A songbook with so grand a claim, yet which
excludes an entire category from consideration, might compare to a book called *Great Singers of the Sixties* which
omits any reference to Callas. Even though pop culture is
more in evidence than ever before (richer too, especially
financially), this visibility too often leads pop-purveyors
into smug preemption.

Accepting this assemblage, then, as a selection of fairly
recent pop tunes, a high proportion—around 15 percent—
retain freshness after repeated exposure. This is a track
record any decade might envy for any category, and suggests that the truly differentiating aspect of Sixties popular
song from the two previous decades was one of quality: the
Sixties songs were simply better. Not more relevant, not

more concerned with life quality, not more meaningful, but simpler, more imaginative, more joyous. Better.

A technical explanation for this phenomenon would start with the Rock explosions of the Fifties (Presley in America, Bill Haley in England) that temporarily reduced music to an elemental beat. Rock then co-existed for several years with the folk-song revival, finally to conjoin with these simpler melodies in time for us to discover the Beatles.

As for the whole song (music and words), high points defy technical explanations: the best lyrics aren't necessarily linked with the best melodies. For example, in *Alfie* Burt Bacharach, as usual, builds gorgeous vocal arches over a quagmire of verse, as also occurs to a lesser degree in Harvey Schmidt's *Try to Remember*, Bobby Scott's *A Taste of Honey*, or Jule Styne's *People*. On the other hand, while Paul Simon's words can stand independently as poems, they are attached to predictable tunes, which also happens to certain poetry of Pete Seeger, Leonard Cohen, Joni Mitchell.

As for meetings of equals, the two most beautiful examples are wildly different: *Moon River* and *Eleanor Rigby*. Yet other instances of words and music which, taken separately, would appear to breed frightful mutations, somehow produce healthy offspring when united: *I Think I'm Going out of My Mind*, *Society's Child*, *By the Time I Get to Phoenix*. If prizes were offered, they might go to Simon for lyrics, Bacharach for tunes. But can you imagine them working together?

In his preface, Okun states "the music of the Sixties was sound as much as song." May this serve as a warning to purchasers. *Great Songs of the Sixties* contains no echo chambers, multi-track channels, voice-overs, nor any of the other apparatus the sleek Streisands and jaded Jaggers used to excite our bodies, whose reaction was the sole criterion upon which this music was to be judged (if we believed the Sixties pop critics). In this book, the songs are stripped to their bare essentials—a skeleton of melody and harmony. That so many of them survive such vivisection testifies to the robust health of popular music during the past decade.

October 1970

Stravinsky and Whitman

Twenty-three years ago conductor Robert Craft, now forty-eight, became and remained the person closest in proximity and confidence to Igor and Vera Stravinsky. From their first meeting in Washington in 1948 until the composer's funeral in Venice last year, Craft catalogued the relationship with Boswellian acuteness. Over the past thirteen years the catalogue has become public in six books, three in the form of conversations, three others partly in the form of diaries. Now those diaries, along with some final entries, have been collected into a single volume named *Stravinsky: Chronicle of a Friendship.*

The distinguishing feature of a journal as opposed to a memoir is on-the-spot reaction, the writer's truth as he feels it, not as he felt it. If that truth is no more "truthful" for being in the first person, it does contain the defining character of immediacy. The intimate journal is a literary form used almost solely by the French. They keep it as a sideline, a book about how hard it is to write a book. Not only France's authors, from Rousseau and Baudelaire to Amiel and Green, but her other artists too, like Berlioz and Delacroix, de Gaulle and Poulenc, have made literature of their lives. The genre has never been popular with non-French continentals, still less with the British who prefer autobiography, and it is virtually unpracticed by Americans who, with all due liberation and collective carnality, do retain a decorum toward their personal selves. (We know more about the actual life of André Gide than we do about that of John Rechy.)

Robert Craft has therefore brought us something rare, no less for its singularity of device than for its superiority of content. Avoiding the archetypical diarist's self-portrait painted in confessional tones, Robert Craft instead portrays a milieu—a milieu as experienced through a friend who happens to be the most influential musician of the twentieth century. No such book has ever been written on a composer. No frank first-hand reports, certainly no literary ones, exist on, say, so tantalizing a personage as Maurice Ravel; to realize how recent yet how forever lost the human Ravel has become (or Debussy or Brahms or Schubert or Haydn or Bach) is to value Craft's diary the more. In a great man no detail is boring, be it about his art or about the quotidian society affecting that art. But perhaps a life, as distinct from a life's work, can be immortalized only when it has been largely public. If Ravel was a recluse, Igor Stravinsky was always most colorfully outward.

His outward color has long been on record, first in the autobiography *Chroniques de ma Vie*, said to have been ghosted by the Franco-Russian musicologist Pierre Suvchinsky, and later in the lectures called *Poetics of Music*, said to have been ghosted by the French composer Roland-Manuel. The books exude the cultured wit we know still better through Robert Craft, himself a sometime ghostwriter for the master. That Craft authored many an interview credited to Stravinsky has long been common knowledge to the musical community, though lately the public has learned of it with outrage. Why outrage? when Craft merely interpreted

Stravinsky's intellectual thought in communicative English, even as he interpreted the composer's musical thought from the podium. To charge that words give new meaning to thoughts, and therefore that these thoughts became Craft's, is to assume that an interpreter can invent the thoughts of a creative man. We must assume only that a great musician need not be an equally great annotator, that Stravinsky was in fact a great talker, and that there may be more than one real version of how Stravinsky lived and loved. As to the present chronicle, there is current controversy regarding its authenticity too, as though authentic art were measured by fact. Since the choice of genre is authentic for Craft, and since Craft is an artist, the result must be authentic for us, because art speaks truth even in lies (witness the royal portraits by how many great painters!). Nor is there reason to think that Stravinsky himself did not sanction those minor adjustments of time and place which are any illustrator's prerogative.

Read the book then as a guide to international intelligentsia, with snapshots of the great in discussion with Stravinsky (often over alcoholic meals): Eliot, Genêt, Borges, Khrushchev, Giacometti, Forster, Cocteau, Graham Greene, St.-John Perse, plus an enlarged portrait of W. H. Auden and an X ray of Aldous Huxley. The chronicle is also a travelogue through a dozen nations whose orchestral forces and audience responses are criticized, along with Stravinsky's reaction—gustatory and intestinal—to local menus. And his reaction to all flora, fauna and idea, most particularly expressive in the long account of his return after fifty years to his native Russia.

The book is a diary in the real sense of depicting Stravinsky's days of finicky order in his own work and of unflagging interest in other people's. The days bring continuous remembrance of Diaghilevian things past, enjoyment of the tangible present (high gossip or the nightly phonograph recital), and apprehension about the future pressing ever more heavily on Stravinsky's weakening flesh.

The closing entries detail excruciatingly the decline and collapse of the great artist's body in which the brain continues inventive, then of its death and burial, complete with throngs and television cameras, in the lagoons of Italy.

In this warts-and-all portrayal of a famous family, no attitude seems too subtle for clarity, no emotion too private for exposure, no musical concept too complex for elucidation. So seamless is the design that it is almost a relief to discover a rare flaw in language (*"Elle a du chien"* means "She has class," never "She's a bitch"), a contradiction in viewpoint ("Stravinsky's genius is wrapped—for protection from musical data—in a vacuum," although the remainder of the book shows the contrary), or a misreading of camp (Auden's "You have ruined Mother's Day" should read ". . . mother's day").

Robert Craft himself remains aloof, all-knowing, while he involves the reader in the very textures of life—in champagne and sweat, in nocturnal anxiety and colored inks, and above all in the ever-present world of musical sound. Since he is able (yet it's impossible!) to evoke that world through words, he proves again that he is not only compassionate and sometimes quite wickedly funny, but the most readable and intelligent living writer on music.

Robert Faner's *Walt Whitman & Opera* is sometimes inadvertently funny, but from the standpoint of an American composer or historian it is often beneath contempt. The first of its two long sections belabors the simple matter of Whitman's musical background, interpreting facts so eccentrically that *Pale Fire* pales by comparison. The author describes the Great Gray Poet's early hopes for an indigenous musical language, a language that might evolve through the folk material and so-called "heart songs" of the period. These hopes, referred to here as handicaps, were abandoned as the poet's musical tastes (though not his technical knowledge) developed, and by mid-century his interest centered in the Great Operatic Masterpieces of Europe. These are understood to be the *bel canto* repertory of Donizetti, Bellini, and Rossini, no less popular in America then, as sung by virtuosos like Marietta Alboni, than now as revived by our Joan Sutherlands.

The second section, "Analysis," deals with Whitman's poetic usage of his musical experience, complete with a four-page list indicating the frequency of appearance in *Leaves of Grass* of some 300 "musical" words (one cadenza, five ballad, six opera characters by name, 77 chant, 117 sing, etc.).

Like so many studies that smell of the doctorate, this one, by redundancy and by misplaced enthusiasm, succeeds in diminishing its subject. Whitman is forced to share the limitations of his biographer. The entire treatise is based on one false assumption: that a certain kind of second-rate music is in fact first rate. *Bel canto* is not serious music, or even serious opera. *Bel canto* is to opera what pole-vaulting is to ballet, the glorification of a performer's prowess and not a creator's imagination.

Though opera may have been, as the author insists, a fundamental influence upon Walt Whitman, the fundamental did not necessarily loom all that large. For each "operatic" reference in Whitman's work there are a hundred references to the war. Whitman loved music passionately because he loved everything passionately; he played the rough-and-tumble naturalist as heartily as he played the Italianate connoisseur. The passion that drew him to popular songs in what he called "nigger dialect" certainly drew him later to the excellence of Mozart operas.

Such vast research might nonetheless be a useful exercise were not the major assumption buttressed on nearly every page by minor follies. Take the question of melody. With melody defined as "based on repetition" (a definition that even Whitman would have resisted, although the author here inexplicably uses "Ol' Man River" to prove his point), Whitman is made to be a melodist: "Few other poets have ever used repetition with an effect so closely paralleling melodic form." If the arts could be paralleled, we would need only one art. But if analogies must be drawn, would not rhythm seem the common denominator between music and words? No mere sentence but a whole chapter is devoted to the melody theory.

Another chapter, misnamed "Diction," devotes itself to the poet's vocabulary, how he used technical words in non-technical ways. Like *romanza*. Except that *romanza* is no more a technical term than sonata. Both may be forms, but have nothing to do with the technique of performance or of composition. Nor is the use by Whitman of *cantabile* as a noun unusual, since that word *is* a noun. Nor does chromatic mean "giving all the tones of the chromatic scale." Chromatic pertains to color. Whitman was usually right.

The strangest chapter is "Recitative and Aria." To show how the poet modeled his prosody on Verdi, M. Faner quotes music from that composer's *Ernani*, with the text beneath the notes *in English*! The author details the subtlety by which Verdi has set each verbal phrase, although we know that Verdi did not speak, much less compose in, the English language.

Like most theses, this one is a harmless game. The purpose for this brief discussion is: now that we know what Whitman took from musicians, why not a book on what musicians took from Whitman? More than any poet since Shakespeare the words of Whitman have been internationally musicalized. An examination of that fact would prove no less pointless than the present book and might demonstrate how certain composers (Delius, for instance, or Kurt Weill, or Hindemith, or Otto Luening) have "misinterpreted" the master with genius rather than pedantry.

April 1972

Pelléas and Pierre

One can detest opera yet love *Pelléas et Mélisande*. One can love opera yet detest *Pelléas*. And one can love both, so long as one doesn't seek in *Pelléas* those extrovert arias or mob scenes characteristic of *bel canto* or *Sturm und Drang* genres. The piece is unique in France's lyric-theater history (being free of set numbers), and in its composer's catalogue (being his sole completed essay in the form). Even *Parsifal*, *Pelléas*'s German cousin, resembles him only physiologically, the temperament of Claude Debussy's masterpiece being thoroughly French.

The Frenchness comes from an understated sensuality. Instrumental choirs are seldom doubled, even in loud passages, while the vocal parts are without melisma. A non-cathartic tastefulness pervades the score, providing innuendo rather than, say, the open hysteria of a *Salome*.

The leanness of the work's each component would seem to preclude a performable translation, the French tongue (especially Debussy's use of it), like French music, being more immutable than Italian or German. Yet I first heard *Pelléas* in Philadelphia in English, without frustration, while various productions in Paris led me rashly to wonder if the

French always misjudge their perspective toward this opera as toward so much of their other music. The most glorious Mélisande, after all, remains the first, Scotland's Mary Garden; nor has a tradition grown around the rôle as around Norma or Lucia, Isolde or Elektra. I reasoned that a sensible case could someday be made, if not for an Englished *Pelléas*, at least for an authoritative version by non-French artists. A recent New York City Opera production reinforced the reasoning.

But a hearing of the present recording (Boulez conducting a Covent Garden ensemble, Columbia M3-30119) makes clear that even if a singer's origins are irrelevant, he must at least preserve a Debussyan viewpoint. The weakness of this particular ensemble does not lie in its internationality per se (none of the cast is French), a foreign accent being more acceptable than a foreign attitude; but the score's first twenty minutes expose the personality and vocal attributes of all five protagonists, and these singers are just not at home. They polish the surface, but do not themselves shine from within the verbal and musical speech. In the Covent Garden performance, which preceded this recording, all except Elisabeth Soederstroem were singing their roles for the first time, which may explain why all (again except for Soederstroem), in dramatic concept, tone of voice and projection of language, resemble students.

For example, though the part of Golaud evolves more richly than the others, Donald McIntyre's portrayal is bland and non-developing, his sound unclean if not unpleasant, his diction careful but still stumbling.

The adolescent Pelléas, willfully self-involved and passive, is also exuberant and generous, as text and music make clear. Thus a presumably youthful-sounding tenor was chosen for this production rather than the usual *baryton-martin*. Yet George Shirley's top is strident and inaccurate, and his lower registers are conscientious but unlovely. If the pronunciation of his l's and r's sometimes intrudes on the mood, his main vice lies in being too cautious. Pelléas may be sentimental, but he is also carnal and playful: wrapped in Mélisande's tresses, he's having fun. George Shirley's young Pelléas sounds old.

David Ward's old patriarch sounds young. Like Polonius, Arkel may be either sage or senile, or both; whatever characterization Debussy may have pictured, the notes allotted by the composer to the king do invite a resonance not here apparent. Ward's interpretation lacks life, timbre, focus, contrast.

As Geneviève, the Australian mezzo Yvonne Minton does the only singing which might be called gorgeous, but only on the staff. Below middle-C she rasps.

Elisabeth Soederstroem, however, is always satisfactory, sometimes heartwarming. Her theatrical viewpoint comes over a bit *démodé*, but at least she has a viewpoint, and her *démodé* is in the overwrought Opéra-Comique tradition which just possibly was how Debussy coached Mary Garden. Surely Garden, like Soederstroem, had a tinge of accent, some foreigners' very lack of accent being itself an accent, achieved as it is by a technique never wholly invisible. An accent does befit Mélisande more than the others, since she comes from afar.

Alone of the principals, Soederstroem knows that Debussy's vocality is not a series of soldered fragments but a concentrated melody (the "spun out line" reduced to lowest terms, as opposed, say, to Puccini's expansion of it to highest terms, or to Webern's ultimate dismissal of such terms), and that it often fills a harmony role by replacing a "missing" instrument.

My aversion to boy sopranos, in chorus or solo, puts me in the class with those "philistines" who hooted the child

Yniold off the stage at the dress rehearsal in 1902. Sung by a woman the part seems silly and the music nasty. Sung by a boy, as in the present recording (for the "credibility and almost unbearable terror which it implies," explains the program note), insult is added to the injury of certain ears. Ironically, Anthony Wicks, the English child performing here, sings better French than his five featured colleagues.

Maeterlinck's play is sophisticated, taken at face value rather than for symbolism. Mélisande becomes an Antonioni heroine, wealthy (as are they all) without explanation, who doesn't answer questions, and is herself not always given replies. Meanwhile the demented echoes, non sequiturs, and shifting repetitions of speech sound as timeless as nursery rhymes or lovers' quarrels. Debussy responds to the text literally, even occasionally Mickey-mousing (despite Satie's warning against letting the scenery "make faces") when there is talk of fountains, sheep, death, creaking gates. Such effects are, of course, all orchestral.

Indeed, if Debussy demands the same requisites for finished performances as other opera composers—good singers, good orchestra, good blend of the two—he also demands more balanced proportions than, for instance, Donizetti, whose accompaniments can be so-so if the singers are sensational. Therefore if the vocalists for this recording of *Pelléas et Mélisande* scarcely approach the magic point where expressions merge and catch fire, the loss is partly redeemed by the orchestra which is sheer perfection.

Pierre Boulez, who knows and could supply good French singing if he wished, has chosen instead, not without a certain wisdom, to star himself in this enterprise. We hear it as a symphonic piece with human voices superimposed. Covent Garden's orchestra is passionate, clean, theatrical, mellow, and tough, while Boulez's tempos are supple as a vast canvas on which his singers are allowed to draw their little lines of tune.

To sum up: The actors do not give the impression of being able to "think French," and thus do not sing from inside their roles, thereby not exploiting the daft as well as the plaintive features of the libretto. This defect is heightened (or perhaps lessened, I'm not sure) when conductor Boulez veils, even swallows, the singers with his orchestra. So, despite what he and others these days maintain about the work's not being a dream but a Drama of Cruelty, the fact remains it *is* a dream, and Boulez makes it sound even more like one by re-evaluating, for better or worse, certain vital dimensions.

December 1970

Notes on Debussy

Music changes meaning as it recedes in time the way stars do as they approach in space. But the meaning of stars grows clearer, while that of music grows vaguer—at least the original meaning.

We never hear old music the way it was first heard; our ears are conditioned by intervening repertories: Machaut didn't know Mozart who didn't know us, but we know them both and place them in a retrospect which alters continually as we ourselves alter. Also, the purposes of pieces shift with each generation: we cannot experience Machaut within his churchly context or Mozart within his courtly one.

History is less a study of the past than of modern notions imposed upon the past. Historians apply their own theories to their predecessors' motivations. Thus Schweitzer, when interpreting Bach as pictorially symbolic, supplies a nineteenth-century intent to an artist of the Baroque period. As for nineteenth-century composers themselves, they hastened to lend extra-musical programs to their own music, that being the Romantic way. Such programs now seem naïve.

What artists say about their work has always been less urgent than what their work says about itself. And what their work says about itself often becomes, for better or worse, the happy issue of the musicological translators.

Claude Debussy has become history. He is already open to reinterpretation as opposed to mere misinterpretation. Nearly eighty years have passed since *L'Après-midi d'un faune* struck Parisian academia as rather bland, while today its composer is paired by the young with Scriabin as someone positively psychedelic. Yet some still live who knew and worked with Debussy; and it seems like only yesterday that he overhauled at least one childhood.

He was my key to France. His music very early unlocked and exposed my innate francophilia.

Born five years after his death, I did not know Debussy's name during my first decade. At ten I knew only the keyboard literature of middle-class beginners, especially something called "Mealtime at the Zoo." But when I became eleven, one afternoon like any other, my new piano teacher, Mrs. Rothschild, in her sunny apartment on Chicago's Kenwood Avenue, played for my unsuspecting ears *L'Isle joyeuse*. That was my undoing. The sounds did not reveal Watteau's rarefied past so much as open a door to modern Paris, which, years later, would become my residence.

Now, looking back, people ask if that stay in France influenced my life and music. But I went to France because I was already French, not the other way around. And Debussy lit the way home.

By twelve, in 1936, I knew his whole output from *Lindaraja* to *Khamma*, had mulled the still-puzzling notation of *Des pas sur la neige*, choreographed the saxophone *Rapsodie*, and sighed at the misprints strewn throughout the Durand editions which, to this day, remain unrectified. That spring Lockspeiser's biography appeared with news about Debussy's cool professionalism and stormy domesticity. And that summer my parents took my sister Rosemary and me to Europe. Which is when I learned that nature imitates art—if nature may include the ambience of cities. My dream life has always occurred, so to speak, *in advance:* not, as Freud had it, sorting out yesterday, but previewing tomorrow. Like dreams, like art. Just as today New Orleans evokes the reality of Blanche DuBois more than of itself, so the land of Paris seemed already familiar through Debussy, and the Mediterranean reflected his private vision more than literal clouds.

How should he be played?

When I still went to concerts Debussy was given in all possible manners, from the icy precision of Toscanini's *La Mer* to Bernstein's steaming carnality, from the Lisztian elegance of Gieseking's *Images* to Browning's "objective" intelligence, and from the "authentic" liberties of Maggie Teyte's *Green* to Tourel's tougher ruby-hued wisdoms. What with these sacred monsters around, the French themselves—Ansermet, Cortot, Bernac—did not strike one as definitive. (When, in 1940, the Bartóks at Northwestern performed the two-piano *En blanc et noir*, Bob Trotter and I were allowed to be page-turners. There was no room for objective appraisal, the occasion being legendary, and Béla being inferior to his wife as keyboard artist. Still, devotion flowed. For had not Bartók, on a visit to Paris in the early 1900s, longed to meet Debussy? He was told: "Let us introduce you to d'Indy. Debussy will just insult you. Do you want to be insulted by Debussy?" "Yes.")

Even if composers had the last word on how they should be heard, Debussy's own surviving interpretations are too blurred for much use. Recording in 1902 with Mary Garden, he sounds merely remote, and *D'un Cahier d'esquis-*

ses is most memorable for wrong notes. Nevertheless, Debussy clearly played his own pieces straighter than Ravel played his. Misty music, to sound misty, must be played without mist, while pristine music, to make its point, should be played pristinely. Ravel's scores were hammered like Cellini goblets into inevitable shapes with not one inlaid jewel misplaced, so his own carefree recorded renditions come as a surprise with that Chopinesque left hand always anticipating the right.

Is it safe to suggest that, just as composers are not final authorities on their own music, so the French are not the ultimate interpreters of theirs? French music should probably not be "interpreted" at all.

France has produced many a great musician (though not, like Germany, a great musical audience: the French public's discipline is centered around the sense of sight which, in traditions of art, requires less group work than the sense of sound); but the proprietary attitude held by French performers for their composers ignores the *distance* that I, for one, find helpful for Debussy, urgent for Ravel. French performers seem either too indulgently Romantic, like Jacques Thibaud, or too lovingly crisp, like Casadesus.

When, as with much French composition, intimations of mood, speed, and color are economically built into the note lengths and into the chordal spacing (which, especially in the orchestration, gives that "transparent" effect), rather than indicated by "expression marks" and instrumental doublings, then, as the saying goes, to let the music speak for itself would be the logical solution for performance, a solution inappropriate for German composition.

(No sooner are the above generalities proposed, than Georges Prêtre's image rises to refute each word.)

Once I wrote: "Because we enjoy Ravel more than Debussy we assume he's less good than; another generation will acknowledge Ravel as better precisely because he's more enjoyable." Taken literally, that statement needs a grain of salt. Yet if it implies that pleasure, being suspect, no longer serves as criterion for judgment (except in rock), it also implies we need new twists if we persist in playing off these Frenchmen against each other. To disdain the likening of them, as one did thirty years ago (how could great individuals be likened!), now feels frustrating. Comparisons are fragrant.

The game's a basis for evaluation: Try to view simultaneously two rivals of the same national and musical language, and, through their similarity rather than difference, define their "school," to the disadvantage of neither. You will see the composers as two sides of one coin. Ravel and Debussy become the body and soul—the mother and father—of modern France. Pair off Strauss and Mahler, Bartók and Kodály, Ives and Ruggles. Or take Boulez and Stockhausen (yes, they speak the same national and musical language, the Frenchman being by inclination and residence a German, and their mutual artistry being the original of the current Esperanto).

Do not forget that resemblance and influence are not synonyms. His influences are what, when disguised by his personality, make an artist an artist. Of course, to disguise the things he has taken from others, he must first be conscious of those things; only second-raters proclaim their originality, blind to the origins bursting their seams. Nothing springs from nothing. The so-called creative act lies in reconditioning borrowed objects, in making them yours, in speaking Esperanto in your own translation.

Debussy appears less the Unique Innovator when we examine his early works—before he learned the art of camouflage. Those fudge-colored ninths shifting like lava through the *Sarabande* to *Pelléas* sound uncomfortably close to the ninths of Satie and Rebikov (both, incidentally, Debussy's juniors). *Nuages* paraphrases Moussorgsky's *Sans Soleil*, as does, more than coincidentally, Stravinsky's prelude to *Le Rossignol*. But by the turn of the century Debussy had become himself: himself in a position to be stolen from.

Now, the chances are that Stravinsky's Nightingale emerged directly from the Clouds rather than from the mere Sunlessness of a fellow Russian. In any case, since no one, not even Oscar Wilde, was ever born fully clothed, Stravinsky seems as inevitable a parturition of the parental Claude de France (Debussy's name for himself) as, say, Poulenc does of the maternal Ravel.

En bateau, Brouillards, La Cathédrale engloutie, L'Isle joyeuse, Voiles, Jardins sous la pluie, Poissons d'or, Ondine, Reflets dans l'eau. So much of his piano music concerns water! Much of that, in turn, is formally his most experimental.

There's orchestral water too. *La Mer* is often called his masterpiece and balanced against Ravel's *Daphnis et Chloé* by those same people who agree that Ravel, in formal matters, was the classicist while Debussy played the rôle of free versifier. These two works demonstrate the reverse: *La Mer* is a symphony, *Daphnis* a rhapsody. They may well be their composers' principal orchestral pieces, though if masterpieces must be cited, look (as with most composers, except Beethoven) at the vocal works: *Pelléas et Mélisande* and *L'Enfant et les sortilèges*.

As everyone knows, water means mother, and *mer* sounds like *mère*. Now psychoanalysts can prove points everywhere except in art. *Maman* being the dominant figure of Ravel's little opera, is it idle to ponder Ravel's fixation on the descending fourth whenever he sets that word to music? By extension, shall we ponder the descending fifth which is the dominant figure of his non-vocal *Daphnis?* Result: a fifth, being a fourth upside down, suggests that water by any other name smells of inversion. Or: how ridiculous the mind over musical matter! (Write an essay called "Making Waves.")

Much has been made of his new forms, or rather of his desire to dispense with old forms by creating a continuous middle without beginning or end. As far as I can see, this desire remained just that. Indeed, despite revolution in all other areas of composition, not until John Cage did the twentieth century see deviations from standard musical shapes (none, for example, from Schoenberg, Stravinsky, or Boulez), and the musical, as opposed to theatrical, intent of these deviations is open to question.

Except for an isolated later song such as *Placet futile*, where the structure is dictated by the poet, Debussy's forms were pretty accessible. Certain *Préludes* like *Canope* or *Voiles* have an eccentric organization, but no more so that piano pieces by Satie which predate these twenty years, pieces novel because they contain no development, simply the addition of blocks, or endless repetitions which, *faute de mieux*, do vaguely suggest an eternal middle.

Consider Debussy's *Études*, which many call his crowning achievement, and treat either with affection (Stravinsky: "[My] favorite piano opus in the music of this century"), with deference (Lockspeiser: "A summary of the composer's entire pianistic creation"), or with veneration (Charles Rosen: "A statement of what he had done, and could do, to the art of music . . . a concentration of such severity that it is difficult to follow the musical thought at first hearing"). The *Études* do deserve great praise; and some of them are formally curious, for instance *pour les Agréments*, or *pour les Sonorités opposées*. Others, like those in thirds or in sixths, are no more "advanced" than the *Mazurka* of twenty-five years earlier: the sole continuity device comes from the statement of a foursquare figure, followed by its literal re-statement. In the *Mazurka* the device sounds youthful, in the *Études* simplistic.

Like Scriabin, Debussy had his mystical moments (which Messiaen inherited), but also, like Robert Schumann, his boyish moments (which Messiaen did not inherit). His coy use of grace notes, like a lifted eyebrow, on the word *nu* in *Placet futile*, seems if not cheap at least high-schoolish, and taints an otherwise sophisticated experience.

What made him special? Formally he was not "new." Melodically he was short of breath, given to evolving frag-ments rather than spinning threads. Harmonically he derived consecutively from Satie and Massenet (in *L'Enfant prodi-gue*), and from Russia, Cambodia (*Pagodes*, etc.), Spain (*Ibéria*, etc.), even America (*Golliwog's Cakewalk* etc.), and finally from the very Stravinsky he himself had so in-fluenced. Rhythmically, too, he was rather predictable.

He was special because he was better than others playing the same game. The game can be called *sound*, sound taking precedence over shape, over language. Surely, if the key word for, say, Palestrina is line, for Puccini is tune, for Bach is structure, for Prokofieff rhythm, for Berlioz en-ergy, then for Debussy the word is sound. Surely, too, that explains his popularity as a sensualist among today's young. For although ironically sound figures less than style or con-tent in pedagogical discussions of music, it is the one in-gredient to identify and distinguish this art from all others.

Never let him be defined as an Impressionist, that being

a term for painters who seek to avoid literal representation. When a musician tries for impressionism, he seeks to *become* literal.

Richard Strauss was younger than Debussy, though one might correctly say that he closed the nineteenth century while Debussy opened the twentieth, because we now realize Strauss's frenzy to have been not essentially innovative but agonized. No younger composer of value came from Strauss as Strauss came from Wagner. He was the last Romantic, Debussy the first Modern.

November 1970

Smoke Without Fire

The New York City Opera last month presented the local premiere of Lee Hoiby's *Summer and Smoke*, based on Tennessee Williams' play, and all factors of the production conspired toward what should have been a successful experience. The libretto, by off-Broadway prodigy Lanford Wilson, was the very model of how to strip a script to the bone without killing it. Lloyd Evans designed expensively lush yet subtle costumes and an ingenious unit set, through which the lighting of Hans Sondheimer filtered with just the right level of nostalgia. The house orchestra sounded lavish and inspired as always under Julius Rudel's baton, while the clean direction of Frank Corsaro appeared carefully rehearsed.

The music, at any given moment, was perfectly lovely, sometimes beautiful, occasionally masterful. No one today composes more graciously than Hoiby for the human voice, and John Reardon and Mary Beth Peil sang their lead roles with eloquence, the grandly arching melodies emerging from an audible and clearly-set text. The composer's instrumentation was foolproof, always full yet never overwhelming. His theatrico-musical layout, planned with contrasts of fast and slow and dark and light, flowed logically through two extended acts. Indeed, everything about the thing worked except the thing itself.

What made it all fall flat? Some of the above virtues were partly responsible, for by the end of the evening they had soured into vices. Consistently "lovely" writing turns quickly bland. Arching melodies are but one of many means for italicizing thought or action, and are effective in inverse proportion to their frequency of use. Instrumentation, no matter how expert, is finally uninteresting when always full; rarely did Hoiby indulge in chamber music or venture into other than safe sonorities; special effects (offstage bands, an unseen guitar) were banal effects. One agreeable moment did feature a singing lesson which ostensibly parodies salon music, but since Hoiby is in fact a salon musician the moment succeeded not as parody but as the hit tune of the show.

One might suppose that merging the talents of our most experienced young opera composer with those of our most lyrical playwright would produce fireworks instead of a fizzle. The failure lies not so much in Hoiby's language as in his pronunciation of that lauguage and timing of the delivery. His musical contrasts, by themselves logical, had little dramatic logic as organic development of the text; the highs and lows seemed therefore inconsequential and ultimately undifferentiated.

The problems not faced by Hoiby were those of linking the theatrical and musical structures, problems of knowing when silence is louder than busyness, of where opposition produces more tension than illustration.

It is not unfair to ask that an opera score reveal drama and add dimension by fleshing out meanings of the necessarily skeletal libretto. Lee Hoiby's devices resolutely failed to alter the emphasis of any character's motion or word. If the libretto is the shadow of the original play, then Hoiby's music is not the body but the accompaniment of a shadow, and thus superfluous to our understanding of Tennessee Williams' touching tale of frustration—a tale that nonetheless shines through the camouflage of sonorous smoke.

The pallor of *Summer and Smoke* reflects the general sickness of American opera. There are indeed only three real operas by Americans that may be considered valuable: Thomson's *Four Saints in Three Acts*, Gershwin's *Porgy and Bess*, and Moore's *Ballad of Baby Doe*. Except for the last named, even these are scarcely performed. While it is tempting to credit this situation to the current managements —the most reactionary of all performing arts representation—it is really the composers who are to blame. Regardless of their musical language, twentieth-century American composers tend to be conservative in appearance, and in social and private affairs. They do not issue manifestos; they ultimately dismiss bad boys such as John Cage or even Lukas Foss (who, like George Antheil of yore, are known only for being bad boys); seldom does one of them try to give the public a serious jolt, much less disabuse the public of its own notion of what opera is.

What opera is, is restriction. It is Art, therefore serious. It is Expensive, therefore cautious. It is Story, therefore narrative-bound. Above all, opera is European Heritage, therefore unmanufacturable from American blueprints. Of the three valuable operas mentioned above, only *Baby Doe* operates with the restrictions. As noted, only *Baby Doe* is scheduled regularly by our national managements. To ignore restrictions is to suffer performance droughts, as do Thomson and Gershwin whose names are nonetheless world-famous; to observe restrictions is to choke to death, as do *Vanessa, Regina, Lizzie Borden, Miss Julie*, the list is endless.

It does not seem possible even to re-define opera in its original terms of spectacle and entertainment now that ballet has quit the opera stage to mature so effectively as an independent form. Those few works which exemplify opera as it was in the beginning—a pageant-like mixture of acting, singing, and dance—are now called by their creators "theater pieces." No doubt Leonard Bernstein's latest such piece, his *Mass*, is strictly speaking the only true opera presently in the public consciousness. If so, how ironic that the most avidly received musical work in recent American history is an opera that dares not speak its name.

March 1972

Lord Byron in Kansas City

Virgil Thomson's new opera, *Lord Byron*, is not a master-piece, but it is indubitably a piece by a past master. The composer's claim to mastery dates back to 1928 when he completed his first opera, *Four Saints in Three Acts*, on a text of Gertrude Stein. When the work was produced six years later, it became, as everyone knows, an overnight *cause célèbre* and has remained one ever since. Though never a repertory piece—only safe soap-operas are that—it is among the four or five or maybe fewer staples in our bare American cupboard. *Four Saints in Three Acts* nourishes through its vitality; even a wretched performance is somehow viable.

Like all art it is rather mad and so beyond definition, yet like all madness it has a canny logic all its own. The music is neither particularly beautiful nor even interesting. Its chief originality lies in its willful diatonicism at a time when dissonance was the rage. Nor is the libretto especially gripping when taken alone. Worse, it is poetry, a dangerous ingredient in theater. The magic of *Four Saints* issues from a marriage made in heaven. Never have two artists so realized their individuality precisely by sacrificing it to a common cause. Stein and Thomson took not only talent, but their very presence from each other. Alone, neither has fashioned a work of comparable strength.

A generation later, soon after Gertrude Stein's death, Virgil Thomson composed a second opera to a scenario of hers, *The Mother of Us All*, on the life of Susan B. Anthony. From the opening drum-roll the sound is like *Four Saints:* always the plain phrases with their modernistic touches (triads used polytonally), soldering the Baptist-sounding hymns of the composer's Kansas City childhood. And always the point-blank verse of Stein's, so ideal to Thomson's setting. The same happy chemistry is at work, though less "abstract" than before, and American as baseball.

Now, after still another generation, we have a third opera from Virgil Thomson in this year of his diamond jubilee. And he has a new co-author. During the 1950s Thomson contemplated a posthumous script of Gertrude Stein's, talked about subjects with Robert Lowell and Robert Penn Warren, and got past the talking stage with one poet, Kenneth Koch, whose marvelous *Angelica* was in fact born and weaned under the musician's guidance, and then rejected. Finally, in 1962, he met the person who was to realize a project he had long coveted.

Jack Larson lived then as now in Los Angeles, an occasional actor and writer of theater pieces and poems which contained a calculated innocence resembling Gertrude Stein's. Undoubtedly the Steinian element first attracted Thomson to Larson's work. The composer proposed a collaboration on the subject of Byron's life, was accepted, and together they worked on the opera for seven years.

Attended by the most distinguished audience in America and covered by the international press, *Lord Byron* received its world premiere on April 20 at the Juilliard School of

Music. Jack Larson's three-act libretto turned out to be hearty and touching, if a bit heavy on exposition and light on variety. His scenario begins and ends in Poets' Corner of Westminster Abbey where Byron has been denied burial, and where he is mourned not only by living friends but by the shades of his immortal peers. The interim action occurs in flashbacks treating of Byron's appeal to women (and men) despite a clubfoot, of his lifelong liaison with his sister Augusta whose pregnancy gives rise to gossip which occasions the poet's marriage to Annabella Milbank, of his seven years on the continent (depicted through an extended ballet sequence), and of Byron's death in Greece. Finally, again in Westminster Abbey, the poet's intimate journal with all its compromising contents is burned before the eyes of his friends and lovers, who then retreat sadly to the outer world. Byron's ghost appears and is welcomed by the statues into their poetic midst.

Larson has quoted Byron's own words when the poet himself sings. He uses familiar passages ("You walk in beauty"), but more ingeniously he has drawn from the poet's letters to concoct such quatrains as:

> Give your baby kisses, kisses from his Mrs.
> Kisses from his sis's, kisses kisses
> Ramble scramble jumble cum tumble cum all 'a hug
> Duck! kisses, kisses. Goose! kisses, kisses.

Larson's overall style is mock-heroic, and not unexpectedly a bit too Steinian for comfort. If our first impression is of children making up an opera as they go along, with fuzzy logic but flawless declamation, we quickly accept their terms and are intrigued at how snugly words and music fit together. But the fit is mechanical. In writing to Thomson's specifications Larson has provided a blueprint, not the real thing. Since there are no submerged reefs on which the music might founder, neither are there risks. Despite the subject there is no sense of tension, much less of tragedy.

The music is pure Thomson. Carefully planned, with appropriate airs and witty ensembles, the vocal conceptions are at all times what singers call *gracious*. The sound is lean, harmonic opulence and rhythmic complication being as foreign to Thomson's vocal scoring as to *bel canto*. The piece is made mostly out of unpretentious tunes flowing from a source rich in old favorites ("Auld Lang Syne," "Saviour Breathe an Evening Blessing," "Ach du Lieber Augustin," and "Believe Me, If All Those Endearing Young Charms" are quoted in full). If the composer seems preoccupied with natural prosody at the cost of a soaring line, with reviving the long dead whole-tone scale, with literalism or Mickey-mousing (as in the parallel seconds depicting an incestuous tickle), those devices—derivations really—have come to form Thomson's language which he speaks with his unique accent.

The accent now sounds outmoded. The *faux-naïf* notion of transporting Kansas City nostalgia to George III's London seems surrealistically amusing, but is quite unconvincing. What functions brilliantly for Susan B. Anthony cannot begin to sustain the passionate sweep of Lord Byron's character. Ironically, much of the music's appeal as seen on the page is lost in the hall. By fleshing out the melodies the orchestra relieves them of their personality which is essentially skeletal; the music becomes less "dumb" than it is, and loses thereby. As for the vocal lines, since everyone sings the same *kind* of music, there is a lack of differentiation which turns to monotony. The monotony was not bothersome in *Four Saints* which followed no story, nor are saints expected to present contrasts, to "do" anything. But that was in another time and place, and what worked with Gertrude cannot work without her.

Thomson supervised the entire production which John

Houseman, who staged the original *Four Saints* nearly forty years ago, directed. Alvin Ailey choreographed the ballet sequence. Costumes and sets were by Patricia Zipprodt and David Mitchell, respectively, and Joe Pacitti provided lighting. Except for the Juilliard chorus which was below acceptable standard, and the Juilliard orchestra which was above mere student excellence as conducted by Gerhard Samuel, none of these contributors was more than just professional. Most of the solo singers were not even that. This was unfortunate, because *Lord Byron* would not appear to possess the spontaneous combustion of Thomson's previous operas. It will need to be ignited by the fire of others.

Virgil Thomson's composing gift has never relied on interesting ideas, but on the uses to which dull ideas can be put. Displacing the ordinary, he renders it extraordinary—that is his stock in trade.

His music has little to do with romance or the grand statement, for it is as removed from the scene of action as cherubim are removed from the scenes they decorate. His music does have to do with joy, never carnal joy but the pure joy of merely being—again like cherubim (or saints). Thomson's lifelong effort would seem to have been to cleanse his art of *meaning*, in the Beethovenian sense, of sensuality or suffering or what we call self-expression, seeking instead, like pre-romantics such as Mozart, to delight. To this day his method of delight is through the constant light-heartedness of primary triads, avoiding like the plague the lush "subjectivity" of secondary sevenths or ninths. One cannot know whether Thomson intends his music as satiric, yet most of it for fifty years does sound that way. And for fifty years it has not changed much. Whatever the secret of Thomson's message, the message remains the same, the composer believes continually in it.

Like the status of Elliott Carter's music which nobody seems to challenge (probably on the grounds that it's so complex it must be deep), for half a century nobody has ever publicly contested the status of Thomson's music (probably on the grounds that it's so simplistic there must be more to it than meets the ear). A composer's impulse is usually apparent in even his worst works. With Thomson it is often difficult to hear the *raison d'être*—why he let certain pieces "pass," why he even bothered to write them down. The difficulty arises from the fact that he is not only a composer but the most stylish music critic of the twentieth century; how, then, can he not exercise the same perception toward his own work as toward that of others?

It is true that Thomson has been a pathfinder, that he wrote our first prestigious operas and film scores, that the prestige lay in the use of indigenous material, and that this material in turn was adopted by more "sophisticated" composers who gave it the slick American Sound. It is also true that Thomson's music, for all its originality, does not have very much to say. And is it so original? Outside his operas, has he accomplished anything not accomplished through the folkloric phantasmagorias of Charles Ives, or through the tongue-in-cheekeries of his idol, Erik Satie? Ives aimed emotionally higher than Thomson and hit the mark. Satie composed in *Socrate* one of the most serious pieces of all time. Emotion and seriousness are not what we identify with Thomson's music, though finally they are the yardsticks by which all meaning is measured.

April 1972

Opera Today

Half of being an artist today lies in promotional skill, yet to accept this condition is to be half an artist.

Avant-garde being status quo, the despised minority in American music's pecking order is now the conservative party. The conservative party has grown weary, obliged to replace novelty with quality, for quality is hard to fake without the props of the avant-garde. And the need the party once supplied—that of antidote to "ugly modernisms" —comes now courtesy of pop. Refuge lies in the sole area not yet successfully exploited by rival groups. Opera.

Confusion about American opera: outwardly we react as though it were European, inwardly we wish it to conform to our indigenous musical comedy.

European opera comes from experimental composers, Monteverdi and Purcell, Wagner and Moussorgsky, Berg

75

and Henze. Diverted by visual tales their audience swallows without flinching that which, partaken in concert, provokes nausea.

American opera comes from non-experimental composers. Our Babbitts and Cages and Carters never flirt with the form; our Floyds and Blitzsteins and Moores concentrate on the form exclusively, with a terseness of language that resembles the revue, yet with a scale of cohesiveness that resembles grand opera.

Significantly, *The Rake's Progress*, Stravinsky's only opera composed during his United States residence, and his only extended work in English, represents, in its diatonic pasticheries, the most accessible piece in his catalogue.

The sole difference today between American opera and musical comedy (which can be tragedy too, as *Show Boat* showed thirty years before *West Side Story*) is that one uses conservatory-trained voices while the other uses microphone-trained voices.

A successful opera symbolizes for the song composer what hit plays do for poets: major acclaim by non-specialized theatergoers. But a failed opera carries a far more paralyzing after-effect than a failed song cycle. Outside investments are too great. If at first you do not succeed at opera don't try again: the world will not permit you to be burned twice.

Melodic gift, a "feeling" for the voice, does not automatically imply operatic gift. Schumann was not known for operas nor Verdi for songs. Solutions to operatic problems are not musical but dramatic. Big songwriters think small, lacking breath for extended continuity.

America has no exceptions to specialization (Menotti's

songs are as forgotten as Barber's operas), though certain Europeans today (Poulenc, Falla, Britten, Einem) excel simultaneously in both areas.

Originality as an artistic concept is less than two centuries old. Radiguet: A true artist has his own voice and cannot copy, so he has only to copy to prove his originality. The act of creation has, in a sense, always been an act of plagiarism; even the iconoclast in refuting the past makes use of the past. But plagiarism is a crime. So artists, who are also craftsmen, remodel their stolen clay into something resembling themselves, and when they succeed they look new. A professional is someone sufficiently aware of his influences to wish (and to know how) to disguise them. An amateur proceeds willy-nilly reproducing picture postcards.

Eight years ago opera was up a creek flowing toward film. It was not a new language we needed but a new medium through which the old language might be sung. Staged melodrama of our post-Freudian period had reached an impasse; one imagined the then-stylish lack-of-communication communicating admirably on screen with Monica Vitti singing what she couldn't say, brimming with nuance that could never cross footlights. No movie opera was forthcoming.

What kind of American opera *should* be composed now, assuming questions of morality are at stake (and they always are during droughts)? With assembly-line pop glutting the market on the one hand, inexpert avant-gardism-turned-commercial on the other, while in between the Bernstein *Mass* combines all elements of an essentially non-narrative ceremony, not advancing thereby, but reverting to pre-verismo musical theatrics, is there room for a just-plain opera?

The art of music is quiescent, like latent sanity. The reasons will never be clear, art has no reasons. But it is clear that since new languages won't rescue music, then all we need is a statement by a great man in whatever language he happens to speak. America has yet to come up with a conservative opera composer laureate like England's Britten. There have been contenders, from Deems Taylor to Douglas Moore, and recently a crop of hopefuls (Pasatieri, Hoiby, Coe). It is not the plainness of their music that seems dated, for pop is still plainer but utterly current; it is their soapy librettos that defeat them.

Art hurts. To select a predecessor as model is neither right nor wrong. But works by these hopefuls are identifiable only as Menotti's grandchildren. Though they are still young, their drama already creaks, while their melody winds its elegant way without a tragic flaw. If art is by nature beautiful, it must be ugly too. Any work of stature is battle-scarred. The main thing wrong with Menotti's grandchildren is that there is nothing wrong with them.

After *Wozzeck* narrative declined. A few high points—*Peter Grimes, Baby Doe, Elegy for Young Lovers*. But Ginastera's *Bomarzo* succeeds inasmuch as it is *not* narrative —inasmuch as its scenes appear interchangeable, like those of *Four Saints in Three Acts*.

The entertainments of Larry Austin or Berio are too random and unvocal to be called opera. A musical form, like any art today, can be whatever its author chooses to name it; yet if opera is the formal setting of language to music for singing by actors (the superimposition of one set of symbols upon another set of symbols which will be interpreted theatrically), then mixed-media acts don't qualify.

A compelling opera can be made to an "inanimate" libretto if the composer discovers the proper tone, as Debussy with *Pelléas,* or Thomson with *Four Saints,* white on white. But white on white was not proper for, say, *Summer and Smoke,* and Lee Hoiby's music vanished beneath Williams' words. Such a text, moreover, being soap opera, was no longer proper to the musical stage, but only to films which can add a pathetic dimension (see *The Umbrellas of Cherbourg*).

But a new species of American opera is appearing, equally unexperimental as to musical speech, but adventurous as to libretto which is dadaist rather than poetistic, situational rather than narrative. And composers are finding the proper tone as much through choice of director as through choice of notes. Dominick Argento's *Postcard from Mexico,* with a score out of Puccini, is hilariously up-to-date with bizarre juxtapositions. Stanley Silverman's *Elephant Steps,* a loud garland of things long past, is utterly of today, since only today can we perceive the connections. If you want good literature, take David Del Tredici's work in progress, an integral setting of *Alice in Wonderland* that is, appropriately, mad as a hatter. Lewis Carroll is somehow a more legitimate librettist than Tennessee Williams or even Shakespeare; his historic location is less defined, less anachronistic to current musical points of view—or points of sound.

Future opera will be cultured Esperanto; not a new musical tongue but an amalgamation of tongues intoning literary works. Indeed, let a composer take some thirty-odd texts from Hawthorne and Dickinson to Ashbery and Purdy. Let him set them, in any order and for any combination of voices, forgetting his sense of consecutive urgency. Let him then trust these songs and choruses to a director who will superimpose a scenario dictated by tonal rises and falls. Let the composer allow visuals that enhance the sound rather than distract from it (a motionless trio singing Sidney Lanier on a distant platform, a quintet of baritones gliding in five slow directions as they chant Kenneth Koch). He will then have created a high-class version of the revue, and sooner or later he will give you, through these distillations, the great American opera.

April 1972

Jesus Christ Superstar

This would-be masterpiece which calls itself a rock opera contains two ingredients necessary to most lasting religious works: frenzy and clarity. The frenzy lies in the "colors" chosen to represent that most famous of agonies, the betrayal, trial, and crucifixion of Christ. The clarity lies in the straightforwardness of structure and idea which controls these colors. The combination results in eighty-eight minutes of a theatricality which, though uneven, is never boring.

The piece is neither rock nor opera, although the reason for these labels seems clear: to pop promoters rock spells money, while opera spells the most intimidating word from the "classical" world—the world to be conquered. The piece is a pastiche from Palestrina through Percy Faith to Penderecki presented as straight oratorio in *St. Matthew Passion* tradition. If it misses greatness, it does not lack for skill and honesty that surpass the tendentious sincerity of most other such works.

The two young creators of *Jesus Christ Superstar* differ from standard rock Cinderellas by being formally educated professionals. Their personal competence glows from each particular of versification and orchestration; one does not sense a producer's mastermind. Composer Andrew Webber comes from a certain culture, his father being director of a London music school, himself a graduate of the Royal College of Music. Lyricist Tim Rice had just completed a serious history of pop when he and Webber met and undertook their collaboration. *Superstar* was years in the making, and the craftsmanship no less than the raw talent surely supplies one hidden level of its wide appeal. Previous "large-scale" pop works, from Ellington's purely instrumental rhapsodies to The Who's opera *Tommy*, have not been intrinsically large-scale at all but medleys of small ideas. *Superstar* has organic length: from start to finish it flows inexorably.

In current vernacular Tim Rice's libretto retells the final days of Christ. His wriest angle is to justify Judas Iscariot's motivations which he expounds more sensibly than does the New Testament. Like playwright Jack Richardson who, in the *Prodigal*, represents the traditionally monstrous Clytemnestra as a logical being in a sea of ineptitude, Tim Rice shows us a rational Judas anguished that God should have created him only to act as Jesus' betrayer. "Judas had no reason to suppose," explains the writer, "that the man he was working for was anything other than a remarkable person and he was concerned that Christ was getting them all in trouble by going too far." Christ, meanwhile, is portrayed as the fanatic he was, given to tantrums not unlike those of the protagonist in Bernstein's *Kaddish*, to infantile poeticizing, to both surface and depth, and to the complete self-involvement of one who believes his own publicity. In short, a superstar. His death issues from stardom as a sacrifice, a suicide, an assassination, a dissolution. He is at once Marilyn Monroe, Yukio Mishima, the Kennedy Brothers, the Beatles.

To say that the libretto holds up pretty well when read alone is to say a lot. Librettos being skeletons awaiting the flesh of music, few are without a touch of silliness when standing by themselves. Fewer still are works of art, although those laying claim to literature are usually built on original subjects rather than adaptations. (The works of Colette, of Gertrude Stein, and of Auden in the operatic realm are certainly finer, by this definition, than those of Wedekind, Slater, or E. M. Forster.) Of course, if *Jesus Christ Superstar* isn't really an opera, then its text can't be properly called a libretto but a suite of poems. As poems they are not adaptations, yet, linked plotwise, they are hardly far enough from their source to be considered original. If Tim Rice, religious poet, is more comprehensible than the King James Bible, he is not up to the style of the New English version, nor as fantasist is he even up to the grammar school versifiers from Kenneth Koch's famous class. What his words do have that is missing from other so-called rock spectacles is believability. His religiosity is neither maudlin nor "with it" but sturdy and genuine. It may not bring young people to the fold anymore than Bach brought their ancestors, but it will bring them to *Superstar* for all it is worth.

The expository pattern maintained by Rice is the formal Passion treatment of set numbers. Each character (including the mob) has his say, and each is granted his more or less differentiated stanzas. These stanzas range unembarrassedly from the sublime to the ridiculous, passing through the touching (*Christ you know I love you/Did you see I waved*), the tacky (*Tell the rabble to be quiet/we anticipate a riot*), the coy (*Hosanna Heysanna Sanna Sanna Ho*), the Brechtian (*To conquer death you have only to die*), the upsetting (*Tell me Christ how you feel tonight/Do you plan to put up a fight*), the pop bathetic (*He's a man he's just a man/And I've seen many men before*), the folksy (*I dreamed I met a Galilean/A most amazing man/He had that look you rarely find/The haunting hunted kind*), the glee club (*When we retire we can write the gospels/So they'll still talk about us when we've died*), and the cynically apocalyptic (*Did you mean to die like that? Was that a mis-take or/Did you know your messy death would be a record-breaker?*).

As images the verses lack distinction, as drama they work like charms.

Andrew Webber's score derives totally from the music of others, but eclecticism is no sin and greater than he have fed off what's around. The true artist has never avoided stealing outrageously, stamping the theft with his own brand, and re-selling it. If he gets no buyers he is no artist.

The whole overture belies the fact that we are to hear a rock opera. Within three minutes, and before any solo voice is heard, composer Webber has treated his listener to a nearly indigestible stew of Hindu ragas, of Rodgers' *Slaughter on Tenth Avenue*, Prokofiev's *Age of Steel*, Strouse's *Bye Bye Birdie*, Honegger's *Pacific 231*, Bernstein's *Fancy Free*, Cop-land's *Rodeo*, Grieg's *Piano Concerto*, and the "heavenly choirs" of *Lost Horizon* which blur into Ligeti's choirs stolen for *2001*. Yet within those same three minutes a per-sonal energy has been established which will crackle for the next hour and a half.

Much of the recipe is accented with jagged 5/4 and 7/8 meters favored by America of the Forties. Here too is Kurt Weill of the Thirties (in the Hosanna number, for example, or Jesus' solo about "The End"), and Bacharach of the Six-ties ("*I Don't Know How to Love Him*"), and Gershwin of the Twenties (especially in those well-rehearsed cross-rhythms in the big choral affairs), and even Tchaikowsky of the Nineties (hear those three *Nutcracker* flutes at the start of the section called Tuesday, not to mention the entire Epilogue). There are Charles Ives, too, and Richard Strauss; indeed, these two composers are superimposed in the final chords.

Why the emphasis on influences? Because there are so many. Young composers often labor in the shadow of older ones, but Andrew Webber is almost as blacked out by the abundance of his heroes as Anna Russell when, in a hysterical mishmash of arias, she demonstrates how operas are made. (Curiously he displays little trace of his British lineage, and none at all of Debussy and Ravel, the two Frenchmen who for generations were the chief longhair lenders to the jazz world.) Where then lies Webber's originality? What is his "color"?

His originality, like anyone's, lies in the ability to take a chance and win. His color is the color of speed. The risk he ran here, whether by contrivance or by adrenergic dictates, was to use nearly all fast tempos. If one can assert that the most touching portions from the great classical cantatas are slow and introspective, then *Superstar*'s grandeur owes nothing to the past. Webber's music loses effectiveness in proportion as it quiets down; the somber moments, few though they be, are the least compelling. Where the text would indicate to anyone but Webber a reflective pause, a hush, he goes hog-wild and chills us. His color then is the maintenance of fever pulse, a *trouvaille* utterly appropriate to the story's tension, and reminiscent only of itself.

The male singers, mostly young Englishmen and all of them white, perform as is customary like the stereotype of preadolescent Black Americans. The style comes to us twice filtered through the Beatles and the Stones, though the personalities of *Superstar* exude more carnality than Lennon and less snottiness than Jagger. The histrionics of Murray Head as Judas are hair-raising, while the Jesus of Ian Gillian comes off nicely as a revivalist imitating Judy Garland. Also notable are the Rex Harrisonish interpretation of Pilate by Chicagoan Barry Dennen, and the dapper Herod of Mike d'Abo who ticks off the one showstopper, a very funny, very cruel, Tom Lehrer-type soft shoe number: "So you are the Christ you're the great Jesus Christ/Prove to me that you're no fool walk across my swimming pool." None of these soloists has a "real" voice, not even in the Sinatra sense, yet paradoxically all are virtuosos, being disciplined actors able to carry the simple tunes assigned them.

The main female singer is Yvonne Ellimann who, as groupie Mary Magdalene, combines the weaker points of Baez, Streisand, and the late Gladys Swarthout. Her tainted purity becomes insipidity, her emotionality a whine, while her idea of a persuasive mannerism is the glottal stop. Yet somehow she brings it off, she *works*, in a pop-stylist sort of way. Her songs end when they end.

In fact everything works, even the chorus which at best is very Southern Gospel, as in "Christ You Know I Love You," and at worst performs with the musicality of an exhausted hockey team, as in "Look at All My Trials"—the trashiest of a fair bit of trashy stuff. The instrumentation works too, the whole event being garnished by a chamber ensemble with solo guitars, by a children's choir as well as the large chorus (plus a special group named The Trinidad Singers), by an up-to-date Moog Synthesizer, and finally by a full Symphony Orchestra (because of its identity with the "classical" world? But composers of that world now write mostly for the small combos formerly associated with pop). The workability of the whole concept, from foolproof title to last detail of liaison, stems not primarily from rare class but from an absolutely professional continuity. And the brashness is more moving than the art; the highest points of all this fervor do not equal the simplest Beatles love song.

The critical material thus far published on this best-selling enterprise deals with the "breakthrough," the message, the daring, the sociological value. There has been no assessment of the artistry of the text, much less of the music. This same situation existed two years ago around the Rolling Stones, and around the Beatles of the mid-Sixties when their style began to be extolled as serious art by a new breed of critics. Not being trained musicians so much as self-appointed spokesmen for the youth market, pop critics dealt with musical matters in an extramusical manner: If the lyrics hit the nail on the head they made music.

Now, however, America and England (the only countries where these matters matter on a high plane), having learned that art is where you find it, anticipate the paid critics by crying *masterpiece*! Not only swinging preachers but middlebrow clerics join the throng, quick to find *Superstar* an antidote to almost everything bad: acid, obscenity, and the antics of Virgil Fox.

The piece's political powers being assured, this essay has tried to investigate the more delicate elements. It will be interesting to see how the projected Broadway production fares. Somehow the available version seems so ideally suited to the recording medium that a visual approach could gild the lily. Still, when *St. Matthew Passion* has been announced for staging next season, it is only natural for *Superstar*'s producers to try their luck. The big sell is part and parcel of such a venture; if we apply *Superstar*'s moral to the fact of its current acclaim, then by its own definition it will suffer derision and misunderstanding. Meanwhile the oratorio, though not solid nourishment in our time of famine, is welcome as champagne during a drought.

April 1971

Copland's Birthday

Dear Aaron: it has been twenty-seven years since we first met. That was at the suggestion of Lenny Bernstein who said you liked knowing what young composers were up to. Although as a student from Curtis I was intimidated by the thought of contact with the "Dean of American Music," you received me warmly in that now-vanished studio on 63rd Street. On the piano was your *Short Symphony* which Stokowski was to perform the next week. On your shelves were *Quiet City* and *El Salón México* which, at the time, comprised the only American music (besides Leo Sowerby and John Alden Carpenter) I'd ever heard. In a wee voice I sang you songs of mine; you asked if "tunes came easily" to me. And you asked about mutual friends in my hometown of Chicago. That was that for a while.

Today I am four years older than you were then. Much has occurred meanwhile to you and me in that musical field we both plow, our furrows crisscrossing occasionally, yet I feel scarcely any alteration in our rôles. I'm still intimidated by your reputation, and perhaps you still wonder if my tunes come easily. Yes, the tunes flow. And let us hope that twenty-seven years hence your reputation will be based on the continuing variations of your vast output.

Such was the substance of my *festschrift* contribution offered the septuagenarian last night after a colossal meal at Essex House. The past—any past—is golden by definition, and surely a certain warmth surrounds all memory of Aaron. Yet the letter reads more sentimentally than my actual sentiments. In *Music and People* I drew as ample a portrait of the man as my needs demanded. Here's a postscript:

In the early post-war years Copland and Thomson were the Rome and Avignon of American music. Young composers joined one faction or the other, there was no third. Both were from France through Boulanger, but Aaron's camp was Stravinsky-French and contained a now-vanished breed of Neo-Classicist like Haieff and Shapero and Berger, while Virgil's branch was Satie-French and contained a still-vital breed of Neo-Catholic like Harrison and Cage and Brant. (The Germanisms of Wolpe-via-Schoenberg were still quiescent.) The few lone wolves, such as myself, were still socially partial to one or the other. I saw a good deal less of Aaron than of Virgil—if only because the latter was my employer for a while (I was his part-time copyist during 1944–45).

Beyond an occasional letter of reference or a pat on the back, neither musician, during three decades of fraternizing, has ever lifted a finger toward my music, be it by performance, verbal recommendation, or through their copious writings. Automatically they were more important to me than I to them—they were older; to this day I recall every word that each ever said, and can realize how their professional behavior has indelibly stamped mine. Yet this comes of tenacity: instruction is taken, not given, and they set an example just by being themselves. Beyond those elements of themselves which were at the disposal of anyone, I owe nothing to either man.

Looking through old diaries I recover this Artistic Entry, from Hyères, dated 9 August 1953, which I still like but no longer comprehend: "To say his music's empty does not imply vacuous or arid. It means empty. Emptiness is a state, a state can be changed, something empty could be something full (or half full, or half empty). Aaron's music *contains* emptiness, which is a benefit, not a derogation. There lies its force. The music is transparent, *dépouillée*, like a fish net that can be used only as a fish net, giving you the opportunity to *see* the emptiness which of course cannot be seen. A colorless fish net containing nothing. Copland flings it, further filtering, over our ears, and the music that gathers in memory is often full of many things including beauty. Music full of fullness is dangerous."

A few feet farther, this: "Whatever is said to the contrary, Beauty is Youth, Youth Beauty, so the ugliest child with his smooth attitudes scalds the snow off my heart to split it with envy. Older people replace with remarkability, but beauty is for the young, beautiful works as well. If I write this today, what will I be able to write at 35? Each marvelous awful day passes like a rat gnawing into my time, a rat that smiles, that wins."

And this: "Escape where? The jungle: I live in Morocco; the snobbish plain of luxury: I've always been a spoiled child. Bohemianism: but I live in Chicago and New York and Paris. Books: do I ever stop reading? Arcturus: I dream and feel sainted. The heart? I've not been afraid. Liquor: indeed! Creation: I've proved myself. Death is no secret either. Escape where?" And twelve days later (21 August 1953): "What is a friend? Someone who could sacrifice and help me (in one way or another) were I in need? I might never need. I ask for someone who will now interest me (in one way or another), though he might vanish in a crisis. The crisis is a rare future, but the present like the poor remains with us. The 'true' friend on whom one depends might be dull, his aid coming only after years of excruciating patience. The 'interesting' friend is there because we live, and life is short. . . . I've seen the creator spirit only twice and that long ago in the enthusiasm of childhood's first discoveries. Elaboration of knowledge, clutter in the mind, alter things; the wide-open door through which I once saw brightly has become a harline. Artists work ever more desperately toward the clarity of their youth which proportionately recedes. Death is quick, and life is long."

Five film scores by Aaron Copland in the Forties represented the most distinguished Hollywood had yet heard. His music was no more illustrative than his predecessors', it was more illustrious. Aware of sound's pliability when conjoined with sights (any sound "works" with any sight, but the sound dictates the final meaning of the sight, i.e., certain music could make a comic scene tragic—truly tragic), he didn't resort to clichés but gave new tonal measurements to old situations. Though these scores have been turned into concert suites and live on their own merits, the effectiveness of the films without the music is open to question.

Does that paragraph hold true? Did Hollywood actually need distinction? Did Copland really eliminate clichés, or merely introduce new ones? Do his concert suites live on? Are the movies so ineffective without the music?

Can you name one film score, other than for a documentary, that deserves to enter, even in altered form, the concert repertory, as many a ballet has? Are the Copland movie suites, with all their fame, really weakened versions of his ballet suites? Documentaries aren't interfered with by too much text and plot. Prokofiev's *Alexander Nevsky* is really a documentary. So is Auric's *Le Sang d'un Poète*. Ironic that Thomson's movie music, being documentary, will probably survive Copland's!

The great Steiner and Waxman scores just can't cut it out of context. (Those of Rod McKuen or John Barry can't cut it even *in* context.) At best they remind us of their source, not of themselves. The most thrilling movie scores are not improvisatory solderings, like those by pit pianists in silent days and brought to their apex by Copland. They are pre-composed set pieces like the slow waltz of George Delerue which haunted *The Conformist*, or like the concerto Johann Sebastian Bach composed for *Les Enfants terribles*.

(Movies of presumably abstract images accompanied by music are unfeasible. Two abstractions cancel each other— though visions soon assume logical shape, as they must, like clouds. Formal sound is helpful for underlining compact story lines; distillations of life are granted unity through the additional artifice of music.)

The feast at Essex House was followed by *louanges* and presentations from the Great, and terminated with *Danzón Cubano* performed at two pianos by Copland and Bernstein with the *élan* of a pair of drunken sailors, all harmless fun. And warmer, certainly, than our memorial for Bill Flanagan some months ago, when Aaron's contribution was a speech, the burden of which lay in how much Bill had always admired his (Aaron's) music.

(While weights within our frontiers shift with the years, outside impressions remain fixed. Paul Jacobs relates this backstage bon-bon: Stockhausen, in New York and on stage for a series of sold-out performances, spots Aaron Copland in the hall during a rehearsal. So Stockhausen introduces his girl friend. "I'd like you to meet the great American composer Virgil Thomson.")

November 1970

A Note on Messiaen

Olivier Messiaen is the most important French composer of his generation. Born in 1908, he is seventeen years younger than Darius Milhaud, seventeen years older than Pierre Boulez, and his national contemporaries are Baudrier, Lesur, and Jolivet with whom in 1935 he formed a school called *La Jeune France*.

If in the 1920s Milhaud and the *Groupe des Six* had been busy de-Germanizing their music by replacing message with means, a decade later Messiaen and the *Jeune France* were concentrating on Meaning with a capital M. To this day Messiaen remains the complete romantic whose involvement quite overpowers finesse of style. His message is God: not a god of convention like Bach's, but a god of private fantasies whom he celebrates as Richard Strauss celebrated Man, or as Scriabin celebrated Satan, or Debussy nature. The Roman Church forms the kernel of Messiaen's being, hence of his art. It is also his worldly provider, since for all his adult life he has been official organist at the Église de la Trinité in Paris.

Like the art of all great men, the music of Messiaen springs from his own set of contradictions (which he may or may not be aware of), and sometimes presents new ones of its own. His pieces are quintessentially French (meaning endowed with a sense of *la mesure*), for when their blinding colors are switched off, a clean economy of means is revealed. The textures are derived from the chromatic ecclesiasticism of Franck, his melody from the lean pantheisticism of Ravel. Like Franck in his time, he is the best living composer for the organ, yet like Ravel, he performs his instrument clumsily. His pieces are mostly long, but only because they are actually assemblages of smaller works. The longest are sustained through hypnotic repetition (like tribal dances or Gertrude Stein) rather than through organic growth (like so-called Classical sonatas). Many are impelled by Christian epigraphs, yet their formal realizations may be planned around Hindu ragas.

His art, like that of geniuses with one-track minds (including comics such as Chaplin), lacks humor. The humor is replaced by an ecstasy which the composer calls joy. The joy is virtuosic, hence public, yet paradoxically it is very private, being discourse between himself and the Almighty. By the same token the joy becomes impersonal, like Gregorian chant which, not officially meant for an audience, is better overheard than heard.

His pieces, finally, are all copiously accompanied by program notes wherein the composer describes his musical devices and their results. Yet the arcane complexity of the notes, though engrossing, is ultimately too special for enjoyment of the music. (They explicate a work as being the algebraically controlled aggregation of bird calls, of rhythms obtained from Sanskrit, of the Agony of Jesus, of a color alphabet wherein chords are touched with red and edged with gold, of theories on theology, and of verbal systems based on labials, etc. Since Messiaen obviously cannot live up to such prose, neither can he live it down; the thrilling pedantry renders him easy prey to pedagogues who demonstrate that his structural formulas simply do not carry through.)

Why is he important? Because in a time of eye-music he is involved with sound, sound never heard before, but whose novelty lies in order and not in chaos. And because in an unbelieving age he has re-given a good name to inspiration. What Messiaen's listeners savor essentially is his unabashed melody, his *bal musette* harmony, and his counterpoint which consists of masses moving against each other, each mass of a different sensual substance. If his rhythms seem intellectual on the page, they are carnal, therefore simple, to the ear, and carnality is the final proof of any artistic pudding. As for his modernity, that comes from colorations which the composer calls integral but which we hear as ornamental: the songs of the Blue Rock Thrush, the Ivesian complications of making many simple things happen simultaneously, and above all, the orchestration that to the eye as to the ear becomes, with its choirs of multiple brass and metallic batteries, glamorous like a giant gold nun whose frantic tranquil voice rises toward heaven.

Few Americans know his name. This would be more surprising, given his built-in potential with both psychedelic Buddhists and with Jesus freaks, if that public were truly more alert than the establishment. But all paying publics prefer dead musicians (or adolescent ones), and Olivier Messiaen is unfashionable... etc.

January 1970

Remembering a Poet

Paul Goodman in his fiftieth year closed his journal thus: "I am not happy, yet as of today I would willingly live till 80. I have already lived longer than many another rebellious soul."

Growing Up Absurd had finally brought him major prominence, although he had been preaching (and practicing) its contents all his life. If he was not happy, nobody wise, with imagination and open eyes, can ever stay happy for long. But he was vital and fertile; more important for an artist, he was appreciated, even ultimately "understood," when last week at sixty he died, twenty years short of his goal.

It is 1938 in Chicago. Edouard Roditi and Paul Goodman stop by impromptu to see me (I am fourteen). From the back room I hear Mother say: "Sit down, young men, Ned will be right out." To prepare an entrance I wash my hair. By the time I emerge they have left.

Paul used to recount this episode as his most Proustian souvenir. I recount it as the first of a hundred occasions where narcissism made me miss out.

Yet I seldom missed out on Paul during the next years. To say that he became my most pertinent influence, social and poetic, would be to echo many a voice in the young groups who felt themselves to be as important to Paul as he was to them—the inevitable covetousness that comes when great men involve their entourage not only through their work but through their person. But that was long ago.

(At the end, in the melancholy of fame, Paul Goodman was admired by thousands who, paradoxically, did not know his name. His original notions, having become general knowledge, decayed into slogans which the liberated youth spouted back at him—to set him straight.)

My first songs date from then, all of them settings of Paul Goodman's verse. I may have written other kinds of song since, but none better. That I have never in the following decades wearied of putting his words to music is the highest praise I can show him; since I put faith in my own work, I had first to put faith in Paul's. Through Paul I wrote not only songs to celebrate Sally's smile, or Susan at play, or prayers for the birth of Matthew Ready (now gone too), but an opera *Cain and Abel*, a ballet (with Alfonso Ossorio), choral pieces, backgrounds for the Becks' theater, and nightclub skits. He was my Goethe, my Blake, and my Apollinaire.

No one will deny him as a serious thinker: the coming weeks will bring homages emphasizing his contribution as sociologist, city planner, psychotherapist, linguistic theoretician, political and educational reformer. All will mention *Growing Up Absurd;* some will talk about his diary, *Five Years,* which juxtaposes tracts on creative method with carnal encounters; a few will applaud his novels (is that what they are?), *The Grand Piano, The State of Nature,*

The Holy Terrors, and *The Dead of Spring,* a tetralogy on
an iconoclast's passage through the Empire City. But if he
was that rare thing among radicals today, an educated poet,
who will yet bring up the poetry? A disconcerting number
of fans, even among his friends, did not realize he wrote
poems.

That was partly his fault. Hardly modest, Paul nevertheless did not stress the sheer variety of his talents. Like Jean
Cocteau (the strongest of his early influences) who classi-
fied his own output—fiction, movies, plays, ballets, drawings, paintings, criticism and pure life—under the one head-
ing *Poésie,* so Paul Goodman called himself a humanist.
"Everything I do has the same subject," he would say, a
quite European non-specialist attitude for one so American—or rather, so New Yorkish.

Yet his poetry is not the same as his other works. It rises
higher, and will be viewed as individual long after his thrilling but didactic ideas, pragmatic and doctrinaire, have been
absorbed, as they will be, into our anonymous common
culture.

Let me stress his frivolity, a quality contained in all artists,
since all art is made from the contrasts formed by an ability
to express relationships between the superb and the silly.
Paul's was not the simplistic sexual frivolity of a Mick
Jagger, nor the thunderous German-joke frivolity of a
Beethoven, but the high-camp spiritually practical yet sad
frivolity of, say, Haydn, Voltaire, Gogol, Auden, Billie
Holiday.

Did you know he actually wrote music too? Not very
inspired, sort of Brahmsian, and technically childlike. Like
fellow composer Ezra Pound, he confused homemade dis-
covery with professionalism, though any well-trained non-

entity could have done better. Still, his writing *about* music, critically and philosophically, was less dumb than any lay-man's since Thomas Mann.

With all his heterogeneity he never became (though for a time it threatened) a pop figure with catch phrases, like McLuhan or Buckminster Fuller. He was too compact for love at first sight.

He was aloof and cool—traits not unusual in philan-thropists, beginning with Freud. He never ceased to in-timidate me because he was, and remains, The One whose stamp of approval I seek; childhood idols can never have clay feet. When the demands of glory grew, his warmth was directed more toward groups than toward individuals. I received his new poems then only through the mail. We had grown so apart that, on phoning ten weeks ago to ask about his health, I half hoped he wouldn't answer. But he did.

"Should we be worried, Paul?"

"Yes, we should." Yet gently he added: "Nice to hear your voice, kiddo." I sent love to Sally, and we promised ourselves an autumn reunion.

If Paul can die then anyone can die, even God, and who can we fall back on now? In 1939 he concluded an epitaph for Freud:

> . . . suddenly dead for all our hopes and fears
> is our guide across the sky and deep,
> this morning a surprise for bitter tears,
> a friendly dream now I am asleep.

Paul Goodman was a household poet, a poet who did not rework verse into Eliotian cobwebs of intricacy, but com-posed on the run, for immediate occasions, in the manner Frank O'Hara would make popular. Two examples:

In 1947 John Myers was madly trying to turn Mary's Bar

on 8th Street into another Boeuf sur le Toit. For the opening Paul and I concocted three blues which John and Frank
Etherton intoned in the styles of Mistinguett and Stella
Brooks. Heartbreaking. But hardly the speed of that clientele. At 2 A.M. Eugene Istomin took over the keyboard of
an upright casserole and amid the fumes of laughter and
beer performed *Gaspard de la Nuit.* Incredibly, that *was* the
speed of the clientele. Next day Paul made a first-class
translation of the second-class prose-poems, by one Aloysius
Bertrand, which had first inspired Ravel's piano cycle, and
for years Istomin reprinted these translations in the program
of his international tours. (And those blues today? In the
back of a trunk. But maybe the words and music would be
the speed of our new clientele!)

Janet Fairbank was a youngish soprano who during the
war years gave concerts of new American music, a specialty
no less rare then than now. She was our sole voice, our out-
let. We all collaborated on many a song that Janet sang; indeed, it was she who premiered my setting of Paul's soaring
words that still so grandly extol his beloved Manhattan, *The
Lordly Hudson.* The evening she died, twenty-five years
ago this month, Paul appeared on my doorstep with a poem.
"Here," he said, "make some music out of this." Three short
stanzas describe how Janet sang our songs because she loved
to sing, how we loved to make up songs for her to sing, how
she is now mute and we are dumb. Too soon the final lines
evoke Paul Goodman himself, with their question from the
impotent survivor confronted with a dying fellow artist.

> . . . If we
> make up a quiet song of death,
> who now shall sing this song we made
> for Janet Janet not, because
> (no other cause) she loved to sing?

August 1972

Remembering Green

At Rizzoli's while searching for quite another book my hand fell upon Julien Green's latest *Journal* (1966–72) which I bought on the spot. Spent the whole afternoon reading it. Or *re*-reading. The emphases, identical to those of past volumes, could have been composed in 1926. Yet such preoccupations are close to my own, or any working man's, not in color but in stress and distribution. By mid-adolescence we know what we are, then spend our remaining years resigning ourselves to that knowledge. Yes, we may come to learn new things, but we will observe them through our unchanging lens. Short of conversion we stay forever the same. Even conversion is horoscopically pre-ordained. Our truths are not discovered, they are realized: they come from within, from our knowledge.

Thus I am the same person as he who two decades ago first came upon Green's journals, meeting old friends again in turns of phrase, in paragraphs rich with familiar nightmare. Those perpetual obsessions with sin and the true way, with prayer and dream, with shop talk (Jesus talk) among clerical friends! If in this *Journal* Julien Green continues, through his specific belief in God, to miss more general points at every corner, in his fiction this very "miss" provides the Julienesque tonality, the singular Greenery. Surely if one-track mindedness empties the spirit of humor, it does fill the mind with an explosive physicality which remains the *sine qua non* of virtually all large souls. (Humor is not physical but intellectual, and multiple-track-minded.)

Green's is a stance which no resident American, even a learned Italo-American Catholic, can comprehend; there is no room for comprehension, only for blind belief ripened for this convert who feels himself a nineteenth-century poet mislaid as a prosifier in the twentieth. Famous French dramas like Gide's *Saül* or Sartre's *Le Diable et le bon Dieu*, Green's own plays or Mauriac's novels, are bizarre for us because we are not involved with redemption, much less with going to hell. Emancipated Frenchmen (the Surrealists, for instance) always deny God, whereas for even the most retarded of American literati God is not there to be denied. (Should one of them convert, he usually leaves the States.) That God is the same to all is as demonstrable a fallacy as that music is a universal language.

(Sincerity versus artistry. If you can locate a copy, read the Cocteau-Maritain correspondence of circa 1924. The poet's grief at Radiguet's death renders him vulnerable to the theologian who "leads him back to the sacraments." Maritain sees squarely ahead, Cocteau's glance curves skyward; Maritain labors for his trust in the Lord; Cocteau takes trust on faith and garnishes it with gargoyles. For Maritain religion is salvation, for Cocteau it is subject of rhapsodies. Maritain may plod toward heaven, yet Cocteau now dancing in hell wins hands down, for his imagination erupts from within while Maritain's appears superimposed from without—a label stamped by the Red Cross. The church never "took" for the inspired Jean; not for a minute do we Believe his Belief, but we believe it, since it is poetry. Still, the myth is ingrown in the French who take it for granted and are less stifled by Christ than we by Freud. The Vatican for centuries supplied a nest for a poetry grander than our Baptists and Mormons could dream of.)

I do not believe in God, though I do believe in the belief in God when expressed believably by plebeian practitioners or revolutionaries, or fantastically by saints and artists. So here I sit absorbing fatuities that occasionally, when they pass the buck to God, seem unfeeling. Reiteration of faith is suspect to infidels: it never seems to go beyond itself, but proves itself only through the self-hypnosis of that very reiteration, not through good acts. A believer is narrow, an artist is wide. Julien Green, being both, becomes a magnet between, attracting the unwary. Which explains why it's impossible to put down this trying tome.

Moved, I finish his diary (the twentieth of Green's books I've read) and momentarily indulge in the dangerous practice of feeding on the past, on a friendship that no longer exists with a man I'll probably never see again.

If I demurred nearly two years after coming abroad in 1949 before reading the famous writer, it was because he was somehow confused in my mind with Elliott Paul! Then during the fall of 1950, while I was convalescing from a primitive hemorrhoidectomy in a Moroccan clinic, Robert Levesque brought me *Moïra*. What an experience! to meet my double in a trance. Narrated in the compact Gallic language, the subject matter treated of American disorder: sexual guilt of, and murder by, a horny inarticulate red-haired youth in a Southern university. New World puritan frustration described via the mother tongue of Baudelaire. Green speaks American in French, the opposite of Gertrude Stein or Virgil Thomson or Janet Flanner who speak French in American, their brittle commonplaces set neat as Fabergé gems in maple wood.

Thus runs the gist of a note received in November 1950:

Dear Ned Rorem,
 Very few letters have ever pleased me quite as much as yours
and I do not want to wait to thank you for it. It is so direct,
so friendly and so sincere. I think that only an American could
write such a letter and I am only sorry that you did not write
it sooner, but you had not read my book.
 So glad you liked *Moïra*. Much of it is autobiographical. I
knew Prailean very well (although I regret to say it was months
before I could nerve myself to speak to him. We then became
and remained good friends). I also knew Joseph and that dis-
gusting little prig David.
 Now I shall look forward to seeing you in January. You have
my address. Now here is my 'phone number: Littré 48–55. I
am always at home in the morning and at meal times. If I like
your music as much as your letter you will have to count me
as one of your fans! Many thanks too for the picture which I
like very much although I wish it had been larger. My greetings
to Robert Levesque. It was nice of him to remember me.
 Best wishes to you and I hope *à bientôt.*
                                   Sincerely,
                                   Julian Green

 (He signed Julian when writing in English, but I continue to call him Julien *à la française.*)
 (Am I sincere? Sincerity, as opposed to honesty, is a
minor virtue, no more than meets the eye, black and white,
a bit right-wing. . . . He can only be disappointed. Or sad.
The wounds of unrequited love lie less in the broken heart
than in the fact that one's judgment is contradicted.)

 On the third day of the new year 1951, rectal region still
swathed in cotton like an imported peach, I flew from
Casablanca to Amsterdam with Julius Katchen who was including my "Second Piano Sonata" on his Dutch tour and
wanted me along to take bows. (Incidentally, my agenda

notes a meeting with Klemperer, and two dates with Mengelberg to go over scores, on January 6 and again on January 10. These dates were doubtless arranged by Julius, a powerful star then in Holland; but despite my well-known total recall, I have no recollection of these men.)

Re-established in Paris on the 12th, I made the acquaintance, in the Bar Montana, of the actor Jean Leuvrais who would for a while become my closest friend in France. He was then playing his first lead role, opposite Mademoiselle Jany Holt, in Mauriac's *Le feu sur la Terre* which I saw next evening, a Saturday, at the Théâtre Hébertot. Sunday I moved to the Hôtel du Bon La Fontaine, then dined *chez* Marie Blanche de Polignac for the first time. On Monday I met Julien Green.

It rained viciously (like a pissing cow, as the French say) during the beautiful ten-minute walk at noon from Rue des Saints-Pères to the three-story house in Rue de Varennes which Julien Green occupied with his sister Anne (whom I never met during many a subsequent visit) and the debonair Robert de Saint-Jean. I recall the rain specifically as a blight to my appearance. Eyes looked down on me already as I crossed the courtyard like a wet rat, so there was no time to comb my hair before the front door opened.

At fifty-one, the age of wild oats, Julien's social pattern still centered, as it had for decades, round individual visitors received two or three afternoons weekly, one-shot interviews with thesis-writers or adapters of novels, or *tête à têtes* with regulars like the Père Coutourier so in vogue then —and in *Vogue*—as official shepherd to recalcitrant celebrities, a sort of upper-class Billy Graham.

We had Cinzano (Julien never drank), went to lunch on the upper floor of the Maintenon, Boulevard Saint Germain, finished a bottle of Bordeaux, returned to Rue de Varennes where Julien watched me drink more Cinzano, switching then to Cointreau, all the time speaking of mutual literary infatuations, mostly of the Old Testament which he was pleased to know I knew. The rain stopped. With my last liqueur a shaft of sunshine like a finger of the Lord entered the library, whereupon my host asked if I would don a djellaba which he brought out, a vast velvet apparel with red stone ornaments and a hood. Berobed thus, glass in hand, I sat sainted in a circle of light, while Julien's voice from the shadows, serene and nervous, questioned me. The sunshine gradually faded.

At five he cancelled an appointment with Jouvet (*Sud* was being considered by l'Athenée), and we left instead to hear a run-through of my sonata five blocks away *chez* Julius Katchen. More apéritifs, Rue Cognacq-Jay, where Jean Leuvrais also came to meet me before going to his theater. Instant mistrust of Jean by Julien. ("I can size up the French bourgeois perhaps more easily than you." But a few seasons later Leuvrais was to star in Green's play *L'Ombre*. By such ironies do shadows lighten our small world!) . . . Next morning a gift was delivered to the desk of the Hôtel du Bon La Fontaine—"*par un monsieur de bien en tenu sombre.*" A plaster cast of Chopin's hand.

Astonishment pushes me to record what seems unnecessary. My old agendas show so many crucial people being met in so short a time! So many hangovers with which I nonetheless coped! Here in my own library twenty-two years later I am assailed not by memory but by the actual smell of each *cuite*, by the touch of Jean Leuvrais's large hands on my neck, or Julius's hands on the keyboard there across the room, sounds of honey and iron. And the sound of ice cubes and Julien's reticent laugh. . . . Today I am just three years younger than he then, and am sometimes prey to visitors like his, whom I discourage with as much fright as he encouraged them with charity. Julien has turned gray now, I'm told. Jean Leuvrais is lost. Julius has died. Auden, in a poem unwritten when these souvenirs were real:

Flash-backs falsify the Past:
they forget
the remembering Present.

On 18 January 1951, he sent me a little book, "the story of a shy boy," with the admonition: "Don't read it now. Wait until you have plenty of time," adding that he had been thinking about me. "Will you remember your promise to call me up? I love and admire your music. There are many things I want to tell you."

The little book was a new edition of his 1930 memoir, *L'autre sommeil.* I read it on April 15 in the waiting room at Marignane before boarding a plane for Casablanca. En route, I translated three extracts, and during the following week in Marrakech composed a baritone cycle on this English prose, calling it *Another Sleep.*

That early spring of 1951 Julien showed me Paris through his eyes. For one who virtually never writes about food, he had a passion for little sandwiches and cakes, English style, and we visited the hundred teahouses of Paris, the libraries and gardens, zoos and byways of the third *arrondissement.* His handsome stoical eyes could ferret out madness through a sunlit pane, yet much of what he found naughty was so innocent! For example, at his local bookstore he bought me an under-the-counter *Fanny Hill.* The clerk said, "I'll put it down as *Jane Eyre.*" . . . Vicarious, he enjoyed my accounts of drunkenness and orgies (exaggerated), hoping nevertheless that I read the Bible each night. Each night in fact I would meet J. L. at the Théâtre Hébertot.

I meanwhile forced him occasionally into *my* Paris despite his contention that anyone seen with me was automatically compromised: A musicale at Marie Blanche's, a lunch with Marie-Louise Bousquet on Ile Saint-Louis, the recital of Julius Katchen (*Paris-Match* pictured me in my silver necktie seated between Julien and Robert de Saint-Jean like proud parents), or my shoddy hotel room where he now saw Chopin's hand, broken, upright against the mirror with a cigarette between two fingers. I remember an afternoon *chez* Henri-Louis de la Grange with Menotti and Julien as sole audience to a concert of my songs by Nell Tangeman. And on another Tuesday, February 20, shaken from seeing Gide in state. And yet again the next afternoon between my rendezvous with Henri Gouin and Nadia Boulanger. Indeed, my agenda indicates a meeting every few days until March 10, a Saturday, when my involvement with Marie Laure began.

In April I spent my first fortnight at Marie Laure's *Saint Bernard* in Hyères, which became the scene of my most productive years. Julien, in Monaco to receive an honor from Rainier, drove over with Charles de Noailles to pass a weekend with us. But we did not then, nor ever again, resume the unset pattern of our first rainy day. A cooling off began. Which is when I returned to Morocco until September.

In June he thanked me for the translation of *Another Sleep*, adding: "I think it might be easier to sing the words if a few changes were made; perhaps we can go over it together. Of course I am dying to hear the music which, I am sure, is very pretty. Has it occurred to you that we might leave the words in French? It seems to me that, had I written the book in English, I would have said something else, totally different perhaps."

A triumph of tact, while stating plainly his doubts! Today in re-examining the score I too have doubts, not about the words or the music or their combination, but whether the text as I used it was actually by Green.

The set of songs, *Another Sleep*, has been performed only twice: by Bernard Lefort in Salle Gaveau in 1954, and by Donald Gramm in Town Hall in 1956. The music is perhaps too "sensitive" but I remain fond of it. However, my translations are not good, nor are they really Green, nor yet me. The effect is bastardly. Still, I'd have liked to publish the cycle if I had received permission to use the words. What words? Correspondence about them was resolved by silence, and my hunch is that Julien did not want to be identified with the texts of my songs.

As to his suggestion that "we might leave the words in French," I can only reply that in French I would have composed "something else, totally different perhaps."

(In an essay, "The Poetry of Music," I have discussed the problem of multilingual composers. Frustration awaits the American impelled to write songs in French, for those songs will seldom be heard. The rare French recitalist who programs an American song will make an effort to learn it in English. Meanwhile, American singers find it more "legitimate" for their French group to be by Frenchmen. I am not the first to suffer from this irony. Yet the suffering is mild. Since few vocal concerts are given in any language by anyone anywhere anymore, little loss comes from indulging the unsalable challenges this precious medium provides. So I continue to write to whatever texts appeal to me.)

On the bus he sits across from a young redhead ("hair the same gold as the edge of his Bible"). When the boy gets off, he follows. When the boy walks faster, he likewise. When the boy finally stops in a doorway, he asks: Why do you let strangers chase you?

"Your letter touched me very deeply and I am glad you wrote," he himself wrote in November 1951. "I have been unwell and am not feeling quite myself yet, but someday, when you come back, we must see each other again."

Cemeteries, which Julien finds unbearable, are for me always cheerfully tranquil. I feel protected, not by the past but by the casualness of the present. No effort is made there, not even by the gardener mowing the lawns, the gardener more beautiful than his roses. I, who so fear death, find nothing fatal about those lawns, just peace, while Julien quotes Maeterlinck: The dead would not exist if it weren't for cemeteries.

He is concerned and cultured. Strangers who write him usually seem concerned and cultured. Strangers who write me are madmen. Disconcerting: The possibility that not opposites but similarities attract.

No denying that his *oeuvre* spills forth with obsessional folly, yet those who write to him identify with *him*, not with his characters, and he, though melancholy and visionary and godly, is not crazy.

(What is crazy? Let the night-nurse decide. Norris Embry, mortally bored by his continuing incarceration in an Annapolis "mental" hospital despite his pleas of normalcy, finally pointed to the door and shrieked: "Rabbits! here they come!" For that he was given an A.)

I wrote him from Marrakech and in February 1952, he answered. "Your letter touched me almost as much as it surprised me. Not for one minute did I ever suspect you cared for me as you seem to now. Perhaps I lack intuition, but never mind: what remains in my mind is what you wrote and you may be sure that I will always think of you."

Who guides my hand? he asks. His art is wrenched forth by some Doppelgänger.

I am clear about the Me who writes my music (with prodding: he loves to nap). That Me is me, though different from the Me typing these words. The composer never strikes a pose, yet I know him less well than I know Me.

Long long ago, toward 5 A.M. Heddy de Ré and I passed out cold while listening to Suzanne Danco sing Ravel's *Asie*. Ten hours later we awoke, the floor still soggy with beer, Danco still singing. At nine times an hour we had heard through our dreams ninety identical performances of *Asie*. That evening I lent Julien my journal—this journal. He found in it a Me he neither recognized nor liked. Manipulator? Crybaby? In the published *Paris Diary* did he read a confidence betrayed?

Intermission. Daily finger-stretching on Debussy's *Études*, and practice on my own *Gloria*, which Phyllis Curtin and Helen Vanni record in two weeks. Now the typewriter's propped on our red dining-room table so I can look out upon the synagogue roof, and onto the (for a change) unpolluted topaz sky. These clean late summer days bring Taxco into the room, sometimes Marrakech, never New York, and flood the floor with dying sun. Beyond the synagogue murmurs Central Park, where the dozen alleyways around Bethesda Fountain reverberate, identical to Morocco's Place Jemâa-el-Fnâa with seven simultaneous orchestras, and here as there the laughing sickly smell of cannabis. But there as here resounds the exasperating noise for its own sake, transistors carried like static-purses, or unembarrassed cyclists, radios on their handlebars, broadcasting sheer din that rises to a thousand-decibel level, then fades as hairy thighs whiz by. I love the apartment and the city. But no American—not Paul Goodman nor any pop singer—has evoked with love or loathing this New York with the same devotion the French singer shows for his Paris. Villon, Balzac, Edith Piaf, Julien Green.

I have not seen Julien Green since the mid-1950s. Between then and the mid-1960s I've had four or five letters, all of them replies to professional inquiries. Occasionally when in Paris I telephone and he says he'll call back and doesn't, or a female voice explains that he is away. Meanwhile I keep in touch through his novels, his autobiography, and through journals like the current one telling me about deaths, ever more frequent, of old friends or forgotten acquaintances. Among those pages my name remains invisible as by a determination to efface an identity that was ever conjoined to his own.

I had committed the unforgivable by nourishing his predecision of who and what I was, knowing the predecision to be untrue. For I was not always kind—though was the nourishment in fact so unkind? Yet even without nourishment, any predecision must become untrue, since the actual behavior of others cannot coincide with our fantasy about that behavior.

There's a distinction between the impression we think we give and the impression we do give, and neither relates necessarily to what we are. Julien writes continually of himself without revealing himself. The impression he would give, in words written and spoken, is of a magnanimity which strikes outsiders as old-maidish. If most people's character is revealed through their eyes, Julien's is revealed through his mouth which is thin, intelligent, withholding and sly.

At the MacDowell Colony I once composed a brief piece for strings, *Pilgrims,* on a notion which had long been floating in my brain: an impression that through music the strangeness of Julien's first book, *Le Voyageur sur la terre,* could be transmitted without words. The piece was later published with a cover of pale green on which, in deep green, the title, an epigraph, and appropriate credits are printed. For his seventieth birthday in 1970 I mailed a copy of this music to Julien Green. But he never answered.

The preceding pages are appallingly niggardly. I re-read them and squirm. Though Green may be the most unusual author of our day, I've shown here not my reaction to his value, only his to mine, and none too well. I've not "seen" him, but strived to show that he saw me. To acknowledge this in no way exonerates me, although the present sentence is a plea for indulgence.

Every artist, to be identified as such, does his unique number. Julien's number is honesty—an unflagging refusal to compromise. Now every artist is honest, whether he tries or no, and for some the very act of compromise is artistry. (Julien might contend that compromise never tempted him, so why talk of "refusal.")

My number is faking the shallow. But admitting to super-ficiality doesn't render one less superficial, only more self-serving. Can I prove I'm a fake? The admission, however, is far from my music, for there I'm too lazy for whoredom or gluttony; I compose only what I want to compose.

A fan letter today compliments me on my "Memoirs."

Between diaries and memoirs lies the difference of years, the difference between now and then. I am incapable of the memoir as genre, as these diary pages of Julien Green precisely prove. Waste of retrospect. A retrogression. Failure. (Yet might not the seconds between these parentheses and that failure already place the failure in the past?)

September 1972

Notes on Sacred Music

I do not believe in God. I do believe in poetry, which isn't the same thing although people compare them. God explains the unexplainable and, however cruelly, he soothes. Poets reflect; they do not explain nor do they soothe. At least they don't soothe me. But the fact of them is more intelligent and thus rarer than the fact of God, and sometimes for moments they take me out of myself.

If poetry were synonymous with religion, poets in middle age would not so frequently turn toward God. Yet neither they nor God can finally stop wars, nor even change our life in smaller ways. During periods of strife when we need them most, both God and the poets disappear.

Alec Wyton, choir director of Saint John the Divine, writes (*Choral Music*, January 1972). "Ned Rorem is a typical example of a splendid musician who devotes some of his time to the church. . . . [He] is also the author of one of the more pornographic books in our bookstores today. . . . God is not fussy about the channels of His grace, and the truth may come from the most unexpected source, and I would rather have the music of Ned Rorem with all the integrity and greatness of it than the pious, awful platitudes of [an] Ithamar Conkey, who I am sure never broke one of the ten commandments. . . ."

Now, God did not give me a talent for church music, he gave me a talent for music. Nor does his voice necessarily speak through any text I've chosen to musicalize. When I write music on so-called sacred texts it is for the same reason I write music on profane texts: not to make people believe in God but to make them believe in music. Music is not a shortcut from heaven, it is an end in itself. For some, that end is hell. What I seek in the Bible is poetry, not sanctity; my best songs are on the verse of sinners.

Integrity? Ulterior motives propel me around every corner. Fortunately, fruits born of bad motives aren't always rotten. Still, some can be unpalatable.

"The Lord's Prayer" is my shame. Years ago I fell in with a publisher's proposal, that if Malotte could hit the jackpot I could hit it harder. So I set the prayer to music, it was widely distributed and publicized by the publisher, and then we awaited glory. But not only did my version not displace Malotte's, it never even made money. And that was divine retribution.

My taste in poetry surely has much to do with whatever reputation I may enjoy as a "vocal" composer. Yet commissioners of songs usually have their own favorite poets. These commissioners might concur with my taste (the handful of recitalists interested in American songs are not, as a rule, illiterate), in which case I fulfill the commission without compromise. For example, when Alice Esty and Caroline Reyer, respectively, asked that I set the poetry of Theodore

Roethke and Kenneth Koch, I was delighted; the poets had both been on my own list anyway, just waiting for the right moment. . . . But when I agreed, as I once did, to set the verse of Mary Baker Eddy, the result was terrible. Not because her verse was bad poetry, but because it was not my kind of bad poetry.

Then why is my "Lord's Prayer" terrible, since it is good poetry? Because it is not necessarily *my* good poetry. (We can concede to the greatness of certain works which nevertheless leave us cold.) And then, I wrote the piece more for gain than from conviction. It was not the setting but the *kind* of setting which is contemptible, for it panders to a a sentimental public. I've often composed, without embarrassment, for the needs of a performer, but the needs of a performer and the tastes of an audience are separate considerations. From its contrived height on the word *Glory* down to the footnote advertising an alternative version for organ, the piece drips opportunism, and to this day when congratulated on it I turn over in my grave. Not that gain and conviction can't go hand in hand. Beethoven did write the "Hammerklavier" to pay a laundry bill. But no one told him *what* to write.

Heaven forbid that I preach integrity. I am not a particularly honest person, I don't even know how to fake it. But to be a successful whore is not easy either, and to sell oneself for what one doesn't believe is to despise the buyer, and finally oneself.

Then can composers write as "good" a piece when on commission as when on their own? They will conform to specifics of dimension so long as specifics of language are left to them. They'll all tell you that hard cash and guaranteed performance are their truest inspiration.

"I do not write experimental music," said Varèse. "My experimenting is done before I write the music."

To experiment with music in the church is to fight a losing battle. If the battle could be won, the church would no longer be the church but a socio-political ground. The reason for experiment is to bring action. The church was never a scene of action but of reaction, making rules, not following them. Great classical works sprang from the quite reactionary promotion of the Gaetanis, the papal lines, the Medicis and Borgias, the Esterházys. Even today the capitalist families, the Rockefellers and Fords, are those who make of art an issue which, being a non-essential, is generally absent from more liberal parties.

Insofar as the church becomes action it dispenses with ritual. Catholics react, Quakers act. Quakers never use music and are the most socially progressive of church groups. By underplaying the motionless symbol of the trinity, Quakers emphasize the need for political movement. When they reinforce that need politically, they do so in silence.

Brought up a Quaker, meaning in silence, I needed noise. So I became a composer. As a composer I am apolitical. As a Quaker I am superpolitical. There is no halfway point. To give a church concert for war orphans is commendable, but no more intrinsically so than any other benefit that is an admixture of oil and water, like a society ball for cancer.

Belief in God once provided nourishing soil for art. To believe in God today is to be removed, to be impotent before more urgent problems. To reanimate belief by experimenting with, say, rock in church, is to underestimate both musical rock and the holy rock.

So much pop expresses extramusical concern, points of view more than points of heart. When it succeeds it suc-

ceeds autonomously; luring youth to church via rock concerts is asking them to accept a diluted version of what they
can get better at home.

Bernstein's *Mass* or *J. C. Superstar* are absolutely swell, so
long as they aren't sold as apocalyptic breakthroughs but as
spectator sport. Their foolproof scenarios are from the same
book that has provided the stuff of good theater since the
medieval passion plays, and the stuff of good fiction from
Saint John of the Cross through Anatole France to Gladys
Schmitt. But theater and fiction the stuff remains, not revelation.

The difference between a church mass and a stage mass
is that one is for participants and the other for spectators.
To persuade spectators that they are in fact participants is
to insult true believers, although the persuasion is itself
show biz and, on its terms, legitimate. Less legitimate is
the next turn of the screw: the introduction into the church
of the rock mass. Now if a rock mass on stage is entertainment masquerading as revelation, introduced into the church
it remains entertainment and thus retains its integrity, while
the church sells itself cheap. If Bach's *B-minor Mass* in concert is more impacting as art than as revelation, is a rock
mass in church more impacting as revelation than as art?

(What about the frenzy of a Baptist revival meeting?
That's quite pop! It's also quite real, emerging as it does from
the service. Pop is quite unreal, being superimposed onto the
service.)

Although Quakers, our parents used to send Rosemary and
me to other denominational Sunday schools from time to
time. That was squelched when we came home and confec-
tioned crucifixes. Nonetheless, on holidays our family at-

tended Catholic or High Episcopal services "for the pageantry." One Christmas, arriving late at the Church of the Redeemer on 56th and Blackstone, father asked the usher: "What time did the show start?" "We don't refer to it as a show," was the chilly reply.

Imagine such a reply today. *The* mass may not be a show, but *Mass* sure as hell is.

Must the compulsion for originality equate invention of new languages? Aren't new accents, new pronunciations, enough? Must we be Polyglot or Babel? Is rock in church a new accent, or an old accent in a new context? Is the context so new?

A pleasure not to be underestimated is a composer's knowledge that his dalliance with King James involves no infringement of rights. Woe ye who touch the New English Bible! No living or recently dead poet, no Yeats or Plath or Auden is guarded by a tougher dog in the manger. This Bible is no longer everyman's property, and permissions are hard come by: the publishers, holding out for a killing on cassettes, make even God serve Mammon. Were this the sole source of sacred texts, a composer would stop composing for the church altogether. Technically a preacher quoting from the N.E.B. should pay a copyright fee too. Let him meanwhile expose the legal eccentricity which keeps this book out of public domain.

Music's meaning, like the language of dolphins, is not translatable into human prose. If music were translatable it would not have to exist. What we call musical messages actually come through words which have been set to music.

Those words used to be of a complex poetic order and highly symbolic, being Latin.

Non-vocal music has no meaning literarily, or even physically. It cannot say happiness, or hot and cold, or death —except by association. It says whatever its composer tells you, in words, that it says.

To assume a need for "message" music is to assume a need for vocal over non-vocal music. The need is not recent. Most of our century's best music has been for voice, and so has most of the worst.

Commerce, which dictates our needs now, knows we want more than a message: we want an easy message. Commerce decrees the greatest good for the greatest number, hence Jesus freaks, the bromidic English litanies of *Superstar*. The same message was always there, but in the Latin masses of Stravinsky, Britten, Penderecki, Poulenc. Today, since it is not music but music's message that is popular, that message must be in the vernacular. By definition the vernacular is not symbolic. To understand a language is, in a sense, to hear it no longer. Because we know what it is saying, we do not listen to our native tongue as to a foreign tongue.

Emerging from the cerebral into the simpleminded, rococo into barbarity, we realize that though neither genre is inherently "bad," both are decadent because they engender nothing first-rate.

Why have I, an atheist, composed so extensively for the church?

I was not composing for the church but for anyone who wanted to listen, using texts I believed in. I did not believe in them for their subject but for their quality.

That the glory of God is its chief sentiment does not qualify verse, or any Sunday School primer would be on a par with the Psalms of David.

The glory of God is expressed in, not through, the verse. I can't prove it, but probably no composer creating for the church today believes in God. If he does, that belief does not of itself make his music persuasive, if it is persuasive.

As for the church as seat of experiment, that is to let the composer—the non-believer—dictate the rules of service.

September 1972

Notes for This Summer

The first problem is to find a problem.

If the notorious suffering that results in good music were a suffering of the heart—of passionate compassion and of experience—then millions would be great artists by eighteen. Music is plainer than that. It results from a formal suffering quite self-involved: the pressure of discovering the sole solution to a given problem. If the problem cannot be disentangled like a spider web and rewoven into the five straight lines of a staff, as by a Palestrina, then it must be shattered like a safe, as by an Ives, who scattered debris but froze the basic lightning in crystal.

But first comes the problem of inventing a problem worth solving. Given the state of our world, such musical puzzles are worthless, even senseless, yet their pursuit is compulsive. The need to find meaning in the compulsion has always caused pain, even to the great who were otherwise happy. And isn't the state of our world senseless too?

The questions children ask us are the same we ask ourselves until we die.

Like the foreign language student who finally understands everything in a phrase except the point, so a composer knows all about music except the essential. He alone hits the nail on the head, but even for him the head remains invisible.

"Your songs are flowering dewdrops," you explain. Aren't they also drops of blood gushing from center target? If so, would you or I know it? You ask such questions, but what to answer! A composer has the first word, never the last.

The future, our sweetest possession, melts like ice cream, so the past, though unbearable, sustains us. Aging into the eighties is the bug ascending an ever-thinner reed which bends toward the ground. Dying is the rope dancer vanishing into the sky. Stravinsky has gone and the world's weight's changed.

When Pablo Casals admits to having begun each day for seventy-five years by playing a Bach suite and finding something always new in it, one suspects a deep contagious lack of curiosity, so one resents him in proportion to those who apotheosize him. (The citizens of Perpignan grew hushed as he passed through: a halo shone around him as he bowed.) He is the layman's notion of a great musician; indeed, he is great among performers, but he is only a performer, and a limited one. If other performers hold him in awe, few composers do.

We see him on TV jesting about Stravinsky's modishness. Then his features turn sober as he speaks of his own composition, the oratorio *El Pesebre*, which he will conduct "anywhere in the world that seeks peace" (for a fee, we learn *sub rosa*, no less immodest than Stravinsky's).

One resents him, not for being a cellist who thinks himself a composer, but for placing his composition above that of others while denigrating those others, denigrating contemporary music in general, yet confessing unfamiliarity with most such music. Now people take his talk seriously (as they do simplifiers like Erich Fromm or David Frost) and thus feel absolved by him for a responsibility to living art.

He appears warm and his politics are creditable. Still, since he is no less *naïf* on matters political than on today's creativity, let him instead become the qualified denigrator of those Bach Experts who enlist light shows to enhance their wares. Casals commands a larger following than they; and whether or not he wears a halo he needs no outside illumination of his playing.

Photograph him. Next day photograph the photo. The following day, photograph the photographed photo. The day after, photograph the photo of the photographed photo, and so on, forever riding the wave crest, keeping that young face young.

Or. Photograph him. Next day photograph the photo. The following day, photograph the *same* photo. The day after, again photograph the same photo which, continuing year after year, will grow wrinkled and yellow, but not the photographs (at least the most recent ones) of it.

Beauty Limps, title for an essay on masterpieces. (Did Cocteau say it, *la beauté boite*, when the dark angel descended the stairs in *Blood of a Poet*?) Achievement of perfection is for dressmakers, pastry cooks, or performers like Casals for whom the Tragic Flaw would be fatal. The hero, or so-called creative artist, can only strive for perfection. He never arrives. (How far can this be pushed?)

A blocked artist is not an artist. Whoever says, "I shall store this away, let it swell and finally burst like an orchid or a pimple," is not an artist. An artist does not *store away*, he has no future, he blooms now.

Produce today, comprehend tomorrow.
Artists make fact. Critics make rules after the fact.

Women's Lib and Gay Lib are diametrically opposed, the one being deductively formulated, the other inductively. Women, like blacks, want acceptance not as women or blacks but as people. These homosexuals ask to be accepted as homosexuals first, and then presumably as individuals. Women want general behavioral rights, not women's rights nor the right to be women. The homosexuals want specific behavioral rights, and, like Jews, want acclaim for what they are, as though the generic label were itself an accomplishment.

In self-consideration an artist must proceed from the broad to the final particular or perish, it's a matter of priorities. I am not a homosexual, I am a composer. I am not a composer, I am Ned Rorem. I am not Ned Rorem, I am my parents' child.

More than Jews, blacks, women or homosexuals, artists in America are second-class citizens. Yet to proclaim this would provoke disdain not only from the Silent Majority but from Jews, blacks, women, and homosexuals. For artist is a dirty word to us. If both Revolution and Establishment concur that art is not among the First Things First, they ignore citizens of poorer lands who sell their bread and name their streets for art. The poor remain with us but the artist has gone, too late to organize an Artists' Lib.

An old game for judging the new is to guess at survival value. Today we play by asking how many of our "serious" works would retain their vitality if the Vietnam war were to end. Would pieces of, say, Stockhausen's syndrome be forever flushed away like outmoded detergents? Such pieces do serve philosophical as well as musical needs, but when the needs become ends in themselves—when they become *timely*—they become disposable. Not the least of those needs is masochism which will always play some role in the enjoyment of art. Surely much of the pain we undergo at Modern Music Concerts would seem invalidated by a permanent cease-fire. And surely much of rock, despite grave poetic intentions, has already earned artistic legitimacy through the music's clean soap-bubble simplicity. We may never be able to test the theory, but very possibly Stockhausen, with all due originality, will not outlast this war, while *Jesus Christ Superstar*, with all due banality, will be around for the millennium.

The preceding paragraph was deleted (with my permission) from an essay on the so-called rock opera in *Harper's*. I have just re-read the entire article. If printed words speak truth to the general reader, to their author they reveal a naked lie; what three months ago in manuscript seemed a conscientious effort now rings false as a forced confession. Not that I am at odds with all I wrote, only with the emphasis. I don't and did not feel the pervading enthusiasm.

What one writes, in words or in music, depends so much on whom one writes for (oneself, youth, the private donor, the well-paying middlebrow journal) that the nature of the financial or otherwise extra-artistic impulse of any given work of the last 500 years could probably be guessed through the size and nature (though not the quality) of that work itself.

My intuition was that *Harper's*, before The Fall, wanted

a favorable review of *Jesus Christ Superstar*, a record I might never have listened to without the magazine's commission. The result wasn't dishonest so much as blind, bland, affable, ambitious.

To see itself through, music must have either idea or magic. The best has both. Music with neither dies young, though sometimes rich.

Good ideas are terribly important. Most artists get no more than one or two a year, carving them into variations for many works. The magic comes from pollen in the air which doesn't always blow in the right direction. In itself an idea may be sterile, even moribund, and no budget can disguise the hippest gimmickry.

Jesus Christ Superstar will not be around for the millennium because it presents the case of a good idea unfertilized. Clothed in lavish if outmoded finery the body of the work is emaciated, like a corpse in a Balenciaga wedding gown.

The words on Stockhausen I cannot retract, for he himself has told us how to feel. What sensitive listeners would repudiate this composer's plea for a brotherhood of nations, for an Esperanto of love and all, when he, with those beautiful eyes set off by chestnut hair in an irresistible ponytail, tells them what his music represents? They find themselves attending in good faith to hour upon deafening hour of static, scared to admit that what composers say about their music need not always jibe with what their music says about itself.

Contemporary culture dominated by the avant-garde? A contradiction in terms. How can the advance runner dominate? Yet he does in America, and by extension everywhere, since we now set the international creative tone. We do so by murdering our heroes every few years while salvaging, in the guise of influence, the froth of their output. We throw out the baby but keep the bath water. (Consider the cold dethronings of playwrights Williams and Albee, and of composers Barber and Copland.) Perhaps this has always been so. But whereas assassination was once considered a fine art, today it's pop art, anyone can do it.

If not Stockhausen then who? It's hard to deny the fact of his following, or to assert that The Young have abandoned concert music for rock when they turn up in thousands for Stockhausen. Yet any music which attracts thousands, of whatever age, must have its facile, not to say extra-musical side, since the majority has never liked to concentrate and good art is hard work. The mass, as we know, is not always right. But it will replace Stockhausen.

If not *Superstar* then who? If I'm so quick to change—or to admit my real—opinion, I am only a victim of fickle times. If the Serious Scene dates like last month's magazines, the Pop Scene dates like yesterday's news. Then how do the Beatles hold up?

A recent review of an intelligent collection, *The Performing Self*, chided the author Richard Poirier for his article on the Beatles. The review suggested that now, only four years after he wrote it, the attitude of a Jamesian scholar talking of pop music "seems silly," especially his sober appraisal of the campy record jacket. Doubtless jackets of James' first novels would now seem dated too, just like their contents. There is a difference between dated and outmoded. If dated means that style and subject matter can, secondarily, locate the historical period of a work's creation, then all art dates. Something outmoded is merely something which dates badly, something whose primary quality is historical location.

Replaying *Sgt. Pepper* provided such relief that I had an orgy of old Beatles records. Their way with their own tunes, their ingenuity, energy, wit, and contagiously magic charm present the best gauge for judgment: the music holds up, along with those few huge thrills from childhood.

The catalogue is doubtless closed. Thus the Beatles will have bequeathed us about as many first-rate songs as did Poulenc, say 15 out of nearly 200, a good percentage. My own article on the Beatles published around the time of Poirier's and asserting that they were superior to their competition, not for their meaning but for their melody, now seems so obvious as to be thoroughly outmoded. But they themselves—they date divinely.

Much of both the "serious" and the pop scene offers little more than every child's dream fulfilled, tantrums for pay. Stockhausen and *Superstar* may momentarily supply the dream more convincingly than others. But from their decarnalized hopes down to the public dysentery of the "creative" critic (himself more a star than those he discusses, a star we observe through a microscope whose lens has been misted by the man himself), all art today is publicity and self-promotion. Everyone wants to get in the act, but there aren't that many individual voices; and while the collective voice may have strength, it lacks expressivity. The stage is at once too large and too small, which is why, to accommodate a majority, the very definition of art has altered. It's all a game of course, and just a game. Sadly the war is just a game too, and look! I for one can't play anymore.

At least change is possible. And though taste may be an immutable *donnée*, opinions like mine are shiftier than the winds. Perhaps responsible critics should stick to their opinions. Perhaps were I not a composer I would continue to fool around with opinions, with the ultimately insignificant praises and gripes about our cultured island, opinions designed to promote my music which I have ever less time for because of writing opinions. But anyone can write opinions, more or less, while only I can write my music, and there's just so much time left. These notes signal my permanent withdrawal from the critical scene.

June 1971

Notes in the Autumn

There are no angelic choirs; there are only the choruses of Bach and Palestrina sung by men. Those choruses are not preparations; they are the last and only word. They are impersonations of what does not exist. Men sing like angels, but where are the "real" angels and what do *they* sing? If there were real angels, we would not have invented Bach and Palestrina. There is no God, there are only proofs of God, and Bach and Palestrina are the word.

When *Notes for This Summer* was printed in the Sunday *Times*, everyone said disappointedly, "Oh" (adding, behind my back: but he never was on the critical scene). When other pieces appeared elsewhere soon after, everyone said surprisedly, "Oh" (adding, behind my back: will he cry wolf as often as Lotte Lehmann?).

Unlike *Superstar* or the Beatles whose propaganda power derives from lyrics attached to the tunes, Stockhausen's propaganda power lies in words extraneous to the music, that is, in program notes which must ultimately prove dispensable. Except that his program notes *are* the music.

Stockhausen, too, has sold out. He plays to sold-out houses.

TEACHING

Kids on campuses ask: "Why don't you use words like the Beatles' and compose music like theirs if you think they're so good?" But I do, why don't you listen! But I don't, why should I, since they do it so much better? I speak my language. I wear saddle shoes.

Teaching sterilizes. After the first year you repeat yourself, and end up believing what you say. I often say that I write music because no one else quite provides what I need to hear. (Not that I need to hear my own music, once it's done, more than once.) But I also compose from a sense of failure, which is probably true of any artist.

I've not composed to "express" myself since early youth. I do it now to make a living—it's all I know—and to keep a clear conscience, to one-up myself. Nothing I've made is perfect, or even good. My so-called best songs seem now an assemblage of concession and imitation. Every work is a new try at what has continually failed.

One aspect of intelligence lies in perception of unexpected similarities, fatal affinities. The amateur sees faces in the clouds, the artist sees clouds in faces. The retreat from standard relationships may seem dubious to outsiders for whom Picasso's faces, Pollock's clouds, become frauds. Others will find a rapport even between Picasso and Pollock, as the mill turns full circle unviciously. The scientist finds unlikely relationships and makes them stick. The artist finds unlikely relationships and makes them *seem* to stick.

Amateurs think about meanings, professionals think about means. The beginner's art is a bull session and his social life is very serious. The established artist, taking content for granted, worries (secretly) about technique, while socially he gossips, discussing art mostly as economics.

Skill is suspect when mediocrity is the rule: good writing seems sheer affectation. Economy is deemed poverty by the long-winded. Now, the core of any philosophy can be shown in a phrase, yet such a phrase (the preceding one, for instance) sounds like a mere epigram to the unwashed.

Credibility gap? But there are limitless concepts of Truth which, if it really existed, would be dull, dry, and sad. A politician's duty is to be unambiguous; his statement need never be "open to interpretation," for politics is a simple business. But a composer is necessarily ambiguous; his statement is never inarticulate, but *too articulate* for words. He always says what he means, though he never means what he says. It is Nixon's business to tell the truth. It isn't mine. My business is to speak the truth.

Some deplore the *déjà entendu* of disks, I rejoice in it. Ninety times, unfatigued, I have thrilled at the identical twist in a Benny Goodman phrase, at a dragged triplet on Kincaid's flute, at the elegance of Toscanini's slight tenuto—twists and triplets and tenutos that were never quite so good because never quite the same when heard live.

As to the intellectualization of music, or rather, the diagnoses around music, when we hear what's talked about we realize that proof of the pudding is not in the recipe. If expressive content in art equals flavor in cooking, today's tasteful music is monosodium glutamate.

Critics of words use words. Critics of music use words.

PERFORMERS

His value lies in what can be learned from him. One performer invests those chestnuts with revitalized fragrance.

Another makes even the new sound stale because he lacks the vulnerability which is the artist's earmark. Beauty must be ugly to last. He is boring because he is perfect.

Perfection?

After a point, most pianists spend their lives playing the same pieces which they polish and "re-think." Do polish and re-thought produce finer results, or just different?

Suppose an accomplished pianist decides to restrict his repertory to one work. Suppose he practices only Chopin's "Étude in Thirds" five hours a day for twenty years. During those years he examines all editions, occasionally changes a fingering, and may even alter the tempo as he apprehends the various ways to skin his rabbit. Suppose after twenty years he has not grown tired of the Étude. Will he play it better than at first? If he *has* grown tired, *can* he play it better? Is there better? Did Casals play a Bach suite or Serkin the "Hammerklavier" better at forty than at twenty, at sixty-five than at thirty-two or ninety? Prove it. Progress does not equal improvement unless an advancing cancer can be said to improve, and how often do our giant classicists force those they interpret to grumble in their graves?

Spent the afternoon listening to Eugene practice his Debussy group. Those French waters literally washed me back to Lake Michigan's adolescent waves, waves which were *La Mer* in 1937, and swept me then to Vuillardian parlors where, muskily submerged in *vin rouge* and fumes of Camembert, the composer composed *Khamma*. The Paris I miss most is the Paris of my imagination before I lived there. But it can be summoned clear as a snapshot of the Parc Monceau, and the sound of a series of secondary sevenths is enough for the snapshot to smell of almond leaves.

E., offended by the piano playing for *Dances at a Gathering*, remarks, "Imagine how it would have been with Rubinstein—although with Rubinstein we wouldn't need any ballet." How would Chopin react to the assumption that his works are sacrosanct, vulgarized by Robbins' use for dance? Vulgarity is a part of art (as Beethoven proves), and yes, Robbins is vulgar. So is Chopin. The shock to E. is the superimposition of twentieth-century vulgarity on nineteenth-century vulgarity. So much Chopin came from dance! mazurkas, waltzes, tarantellas, polonaises. Other of his music is sprung from acts of motion: a Barcarolle to inspire boat rowers, a Berceuse to accompany cradle-rockers. You say these forms have been stylized by Chopin? Must they be heard only in recital by rows of motionless freaks? Is it corrupting to move with the sound? The highest compliment a composer can hear: you make me want to sing and dance. All music, from the burial hymns of old Egypt to the urbanities of Varèse, rises from the vocal cords and from the human torso in contraction and release. And musical performance that does not provoke kinetic response is not worth the trouble.

Shirley is distressed when I say that the best music must be nasty as well as beautiful, that it partakes of the gutter as of the altar. It is not a question of whether Beethoven took from the gutter, but of whether the gutter is bad. For Shirley it's bad. For me it's just another place. Gregorian chant had the best of both possible worlds.

There's good music with charm but no character: Federico Mompou, Reynaldo Hahn, John Gruen. There's good music with character but no charm: Beethoven, Bruckner, Berlioz. There's good music with both: Chopin, Falla, Moussorgsky. Now the music with both is not generally considered the greatest. Is there good music with neither?

To place Beethoven on a pedestal is to miss his point. Place Reynaldo Hahn there instead, for he was ethereal and removed. Beethoven is too all-embracing for the preciosity of pedestals.

The looks of a performer while performing prove something. If he is the real thing, though otherwise ugly, he will project an appeal while playing. An artist at his easel oozes sex. Concentration on something not himself is a composer's one refuge from ego, and only a body freed of ego can bear scrutiny. Such carnal purity is never apparent on the faces of audiences at concerts or galleries who display the stupor of ecstasy or just plain boredom; nor is it apparent in second-rate performers who, with their respect of art, are simply worshipful, hence ego-ridden.

Narcissus was not sensual. Heaven forbid that genius not be ego-oriented! But the *act* of genius is selfless.

(Yet in my old diaries I find the following entries: "Amsterdam, 1951. With great sweetness Julius [Katchen] says that he can never play the Andante of Brahms F-minor Sonata without an erection, and once during a concert he quite literally came."

"1958. Visit to Mitropoulos, New York Hospital. . . . He maintains that the orchestra members are his children, his 'barnyard of chicks,' whom he fucks collectively at each performance.")

JH for a decade pondered Messiaen's *La Nativité*. Now he proposes to omit an added sixth in one of the final chords, on the grounds that Messiaen would no longer hold to such a cliché. Yet that added sixth may be just what Messiaen most clings to, and has never questioned.

It is not trashiness which an artist rejects, or even sees, in his own work so much as loose seams. He may hate the frame, not the picture. Nothing is riskier than to ingratiate yourself with an artist by showing that you love his work enough to suggest improvements.

HEARING

We do not know how music of the distant past was heard, nor yet of the recent past, nor do we even know how current friends hear single sounds, much less how they hear phrases. We can compare performances, we can define differences between them, but not how we are hearing them.

I love David Del Tredici's new wild *Pot Pourri* for chorus, soprano, rock band, and large orchestra. But what I love there he ignores. I hear long lines where he intends jerks, laughs where he asks for tears. Elsewhere he uses intact Bach's *Es ist genug*. Ever since Berg's fiddle concerto—which David professes not to know—brought us this chorale, it has beguiled me, *not* for those "enigmatic" progressions but for the straightforward jazz of measures 12–14. The third beat of measure 13 is clearly a blue note, if the phrase is heard as E-major. To David who hears the phrase in A, that beat is a mere subdominant. If *we* hear it differently, how then did Berg hear it? or Bach himself, who never knew the blues? We four composers may agree only as to the chorale's value, not its character.

We are more unanimous about the fact of merit than about the nature of merit. Tuning in on a Haydnistic piece we've never heard, we're sure it can't be Haydn, not because of the style but because of the quality. You and I concur on that quality but listen to it differently. Good music seems absolute, retaining goodness through myriad massacres.

My first compositional *trouvailles* were notations of misreadings of Bach. To this day the forty-seventh bar of the second movement of Mozart's K. 309 is pure *Salome*, since I learned that Sonata the same week I first heard Strauss's opera.

All of us hear all music by comparing it to all the other music in our ken. Such comparison is colored according to the time-space between juxtapositions. If we don't *know* any music beyond what we are presently hearing, our experience is clearly narrow—the case with, say, most rock freaks.

(Develop these ideas. Though is there more to say?)

WORKING

My *donnée* or raw notion—the spark that's lit in the night —usually ends up as an accompaniment. If the notion is for a song, it's offered gratis as a canvas on which I must later paint the melody. Orchestral notions given in dreams are for sonorities, not ideas: a gift of background. Conscious sweat pays dearly for the foreground.

I can't remember how I wrote this or that. Even if I could, the secret must stay mine. A composer's methods are personal, no matter how public he would make them. For the public, what he tried to do is less pertinent than what he did do.

If the span of a second contains indivisible billions of segments, and each segment contains indivisible billions of segments forever, a life can be measured by the width of a thought. But we humans standing apart from this hive are impotent to catch and sustain one such segment, for, except under drugs, we can't freeze time. The greatest composer, like the least, concocts his music not according to sonority but according to time, and his concept of time is rough compared to the philosopher's, the theoretician's. Bach's seconds, not "infinite" but gross, are conceived to be perceived and relished in relation to each other, as a flow. (The flow, of course, exists only for some, passing in one ear and out the other of others.)

Possibly a composer's whole *oeuvre* balances in some way his metabolic pace. For instance, Fauré never wrote intrinsically fast music; his fast music is really slow music speeded up.

People sometimes ask why I don't set myself to music. I set words to music I feel can take a change. As a composer of songs I don't seek to improve words so much as to re-emphasize them—to alter their dimension. Music can't heighten the meaning of words, only change their meaning (unless to heighten be a form of change). Occasionally the words benefit from the change; but although they might not inherently *need* this change, I must feel that they need it.

Now, to write words with the intention of setting them would be to write words I intended by definition to change. Only a bad text could emerge from so inhibiting a task. Nor could I musicalize words I had written at another time and for their own sake, since those words would not exist if I had been able (at that other time) to express their sense in music. As for composing words and music simultaneously, that is a game for precocious children, and presupposes a third party beneath the skin of the composer-poet: the performer. Balladeers are triple personalities dealing in short forms (or repetitious narratives). The mere dual personality, or non-performing composer-writer, usually deals in large librettos which he writes as he goes along. Menotti, Blitzstein, Tippett, Nono.

There is already a presumption in a composer who sets a poet to music. To direct this presumption toward his own prose would be presumptuousissimo.

In writing vocal music I have never used special effects—no whines, shrieks, whispers, elongations, nor even word repetitions. My aim toward poetry is, I suppose, to intensify rather than to reinterpret.

In a word, my music is expressivity—rather than novelty. Expressivity is not novel, nor is novelty ever expressive. Yet this is my one trump card, which will either save or sink me, and, being naked, I'm more vulnerable than most these days.

POETICIZING

My need for poetry is utilitarian. I read it not for pleasure but to keep abreast of friends' work or to seek texts for music. I don't dislike poetry, though it is hard for me. Because I cannot understand it I make songs of it. (Did Schumann need poetry for itself alone?)

The only thing bad about songs in English is bad English.

At a party I tell John Ashbery that, having recovered from a love affair, I don't intend to start over. "I'm tired of being shit on."

With concerned disbelief John replies, "You *are*?"

At a party I run into Kenneth Koch for the first time in years. "Haven't seen you in a coon's age."

With an open smile Kenneth replies, "It's been longer than that."

After the party for *The Paris Diary* Frank O'Hara tells Joe LeSueur who tells Joe Adamiak who tells me that my journal "reads like *The Alice B. Toklas Cook Book* without the recipes."

The verbal style of the so-called New York poets resembles to a T their written style. They speak to everyone including each other as though reciting lines from their own plays. Because, precisely, this style attracts me while excluding me, I take revenge (like the cuckoo who lays her eggs in other people's nests) by setting the style to music. Each setting provokes a grave contretemps with the poet, while the few remaining poets I've not set implore me.

SINGING

To Juilliard for part of Callas's master class. She is, for me, the sole diva ever to perform meaningfully a meaningless repertory. From the moment she strode onto that Roman stage in 1954 and intoned the words *È forse qui* I've been no less enamored of her than has your average opera queen who knows far more than I.

Yet how can a star teach, except by doing? What Callas imparts (through her handsome mock-humble style of Regular Gal, no-nonsense, let's-get-down-to-work—and she's a dead ringer for Rosemarie Beck) is not more exceptional than what any intelligence imparts: Pretend you understand the words, sing them like you mean them. Alan Rich seemed impressed by her advice for hitting a high C: "Think B!" Why not think D-flat? But I'm not a singer. And not being a singer I learned little, for how much nuance can be disclosed in Bellini?

(I say this, who would not permit some other to say it. I compose song, and my business is not tolerance but self-protection. Stick to contemporary music, mesdames: those fierce roulades in Mozart will wreck your voice!)

No music of any period, when a singer learns to like it, can harm his voice. He must perform the music of his own time to keep in trim for those risky skips in *bel canto* which will otherwise kill him.

Bel canto is the pap of the past as pop is the pap of the present. Being a mere gymnastic sketch, *bel canto* contains nothing not more commendably contained in Bach or Mozart. By stressing the doing over what's done, the shadow before the substance, *bel canto* utterly embodies the superficial. What intellect can admire, for itself on the page unsung, the hurdy-gurdyisms of a Donizetti? Maria Callas, like Billie Holiday, gave sense to senseless airs, but what is that music without the diva? Bad music needs interpretation, good music plays itself.

Nor that *bel canto* is wholly bad, just too big for itself. Like Albert Schweitzer or Zen, like Bob Dylan or Scientology, like Toscanini or Structuralism, *bel canto* is obscenely merchandized. If the past season's Philharmonic display overrated Liszt for his underratedness, the reverse holds for *bel canto*.

People often compare Bessie and Billie as though they were the same thing, like Bardot and Brigitte, or as though they could be blended, like benedictine and brandy. In fact, they were not even chipped off the same old block. Bessie Smith was a big-scale rural belter of Negro-oriented song. Billie Holiday was a small-scale urban "stylist" of songs by white masters. Bessie, a born leader, sang blues. Billie, a born victim, sang pop. Sure, they're comparable, in quality and society, since both were great black vocalists. But generically they're as different as an outdoor stadium and a supper club, different as a Wagnerian diva and a lieder singer.

More than other vocal pigeonholes mezzo-soprano neatly splits in two: the soft sound and the hard. Some are contraltos with a top and make chocolate noises associated with deep sensuality. Others are sopranos with a bottom and make diamond noises identified with high purity.

Britten may be a "lesser" composer than Stravinsky. The fact remains that to vote between the single most extended work (as the clock ticks) of each man, *Peter Grimes* and *The Rake*, is to elect *Peter Grimes*. Britten's opera in all ways surpasses Stravinsky's: technically, coloristically, literarily, and operatically. It is more rewarding for singers, more "inspired," more moving. If both pieces are pastiches —and they are—Britten's works and Stravinsky's doesn't. Which is not to say that *Grimes* is superior to *Sacre*. But staged opera was not Stravinsky's forte. *Rossignol* and *Mavra* are his weakest scores.

HUMOR

Our cousins, Chester Ronning and his daughter Audrey Topping, came with my parents to dine last night. (Famous spiced chicken, plus Grimble's cheesecake with a hot strawberry sauce.) Chester and my father, both seventy-seven, look fifty-nine, and suave Audrey in white leather, blondined and booted, hardly seemed smack out of Communist territories. But both, though Norwegian capitalists, are Chinese linguists and, by now, cool and collected with interviewers. After supper Eugene Istomin came over with John Trapp and we took family pictures.

Chester, asked no doubt for the millionth time what humor is like in China, replies it's like anywhere else, and illustrates with a joke: A henpecked husband, fed up, exclaims, "I'll die before I let her get away with this anymore," whereupon he drops dead. Now that's not funny in itself, nor hardly just Chinese, the figurative-as-literal being one of the four basic devices of all times.

But there *is* rich-people wit and poor-people wit, French humor and Jewish humor. People *are* different, with their ethnic and national fun, primitive and sophisticated fun. Humor is not exemplified in The Funny Story, since there are too many ways to relate that same plot. Humor is tone based on irony, a Janus head. Children, being literal-minded, have no humor. Which doesn't mean they're pedestrian: they literally see a blue elephant flying, a candy house, Santa Claus. Humor will come to them with disillusionment. By this definition the Chinese peasant probably lacks humor since he lacks training in the nuance of contrast—at least in *our* nuance of contrast.

French: brevity. Jokes about cuckolds.

German: drawn out ("German jokes are no laughing matter"). About food and scatology.

American: sex.

Did Handel have humor? His music's too removed to assess in perspective. Perhaps he was not even great. How long does greatness last?

What *is* musical humor? How wearying to hear forever about Haydn's wit. Play him with a movie on childbirth (as Cocteau played Bach for a suicide) and you'll hear how witty he is!

If Chopin's tunes were better (funnier) than Beethoven's, was he greater than Beethoven?

Have I said all this better elsewhere?

All great art contains humor. Insofar as Beethoven lacked humor he lacked greatness. Children and the insane lack the irony of humor. Ironically, the great are sometimes called grownup children. They are not. They are like everyone else only more so—like everyone else, but no one is like them.

Humor means seeing three sides of one coin.

Hall Overton's *Huckleberry Finn* failed utterly and for the same reason as my *Miss Julie*, these operas being two sides of one coin. Both composers miscalculated their language: Overton chose chromatic speech for an essentially uncomplicated exterior situation, while my speech was diatonic for a complex inner situation.

Dodecaphonism, inherently tense, has built in too many humorless Luluesque associations to be usable for a Mark Twain book despite its updating to center on Nigger Jim, while diatonicism, inherently relaxed, is incapable of illustrating madness, at least current madness (and Strindberg is more current than Twain). In theater style is all. Even calculated misplacements are risky.

Thus neither Overton nor I by nature of our language could translate the subject matter. Had we traded librettos we might have hit the jackpot.

Fakery in opera is more discernible than in other modern music's modes. Being so slippery in so many ways, particularly in reliance on words, opera cannot depend on rhetoric rather than on expressivity. Opera *must* depend on expressivity. It is hard to imagine one by Stockhausen, since he depends on philosophy, on extramusicality.

LOU'S BOOK

A newish composer, George Crumb, has lately received much acclaim for his (let's call them) sonorous canvases—skillfully stretched sheets of sound effects offered as ends in themselves. Well, for thirty-five years another composer, Lou Harrison, has been concocting similar backgrounds, with the added difference that he paints pretty tunes upon them. Crumb is Harrison without the tunes, but younger and so newsworthy. But Harrison has now come out with a sort of book. If it won't exactly make him a star, it will add light to his special obscurity.

Music Primer is a fifty-page handwritten notebook of everything this composer knows about being a composer. The knowledge is dispensed so engagingly that the book makes an ideal gift for precious young people weary of cornball Music Appreciation texts. Harrison is a composer who, in a language you can understand, tells you how to compose. There are pages of crystalline maxims, earthy advice, and charts of exercises geared to start off a pupil immediately on the creation of music rather than theory.

A portion of these maxims forms Harrison's version of Eastern wisdom ("Chinese opera is complete musical theater, for it includes and offers all that can be done with text and music. Plain speech, unaccompanied. Rhythmicized speech accompanied. Song unaccompanied, etc., up to and including Chorus accompanied.") He spent years in Korea and the results of his study there are shown through the music itself rather than through talk about the music. In Orientology Harrison is the most informed Western composer since the lamented Henry Cowell. He is practical too ("There are really four kinds of composition: Voluntary, Suggested, Requested, Commissioned. Best of all is when someone commissions an already begun voluntary work!"), and thrillingly indignant, as when dissecting copyright ("If the public deems our works sufficiently valuable to go to the trouble to claim them by laws, then why does it not 'Keep' us, or recompense us in the manner indicated? Instead it seems to fancy that our greatest desire, even Need, is to Please it!").

Harrison is one of the most original composers today, right in the American grain of Charles Ives and Harry Partch.

You won't find *Music Primer* in stores, but for four dollars you can order it directly from the music publishers, C. F. Peters, Inc., 373 Park Avenue South, New York, N.Y. 10016.

A last charming quote: "The 'correct' music is usually swept away by musicians impatient to make music in their own way. Once formed and correctly notated, Gregorian Chant soon lost its rhythms and then its tunes. Today the younger European-style composers often abandon precise notation or even precise forming and 'give it all back to' the performer. This is very understandable—the young are no longer much allowed to plan their lives; why should they plan their music?" Well, Lou Harrison's book is an attractive reason why. And it's ever so gay, in the Yeatsian sense that all art, whatever its subject, by being regenerative, or just by being, is optimistic.

May 1972